This Is My Story

This Is My Story

I.V. White

This Is My Story
© 2011 by I.V. White

This book or parts thereof may not be reproduced in any form, stored in a retrieval system, or transmitted in any form by any means—electronic, mechanical, photocopy, recording, or otherwise—without prior written permission of the publisher, except as provided by United States of America copyright law.

Copyright © 2011 by I.V. White
All rights reserved

All Scripture quotations are from the King James Version of the Bible.

Cover Design and Layout: Cathleen Kwas

ISBN: 978-0-9820475-8-3
Printed in the United States of America

I dedicate this book to my six children, Emanuel, Gary, George, Isaac, Endia and especially Olivia Berniece White, who went home to live with Jesus in 1996.

It's my hope that the life I've lived will always be an example and much encouragement to them. And may I say here, for the many headaches they gave me, I've been rewarded 100 times over. Again, I want you to know how thankful I am.

Rebecca and I.V. White

TABLE OF CONTENTS

	Preface	ix
	Acknowledgements	xiii
Introduction	In the Beginning	1
Chapter 1	Planting My First Congregation	9
Chapter 2	The Conversion of Momma	21
Chapter 3	My Greatest	29
Chapter 4	A Vessel of God	33
Chapter 5	Be Sure Your Sins Will Find You Out	43
Chapter 6	Building for Eternity	55
Chapter 7	Baptism	69
Chapter 8	God's People Develop Water-Walking Faith	77
Chapter 9	Patience	85
Chapter 10	Rightly Dividing	95
	About the Author	105

PREFACE

EVERYONE IS FAMILIAR WITH THE AGE-OLD-adage, "we only have one life to live." Unfortunately, not everyone gets to live that life to the fullest. Some spend life searching for an identity, pursuing vices and devices to discover who they are, whose they are, and who they desire to become.

Many become "caught up" on a quest for financial riches, and miss-out on the simple treasures of life: subsequently, creating for themselves unnecessary hardships, undergoing financial suffering and social setbacks, succumbing to the kinds of stress that cause men heart attacks, and becoming mentally abducted and victims of a psychological kidnap. Most people fail to learn what makes a life complete, due to spiritual throwbacks.

The aim of this book is to highlight the triumphs and achievements, as well as the difficulties and the plight, found in a single human story. Because every life should have meaning, it is the hope of the author, while chronicling his life, to offer his perspective of the meaning of life, in hopes to influence the hearts of "some" with his story.

A "story" is a narrative re-accounting a sequence of events, using methods that illustrate ideas: ideas designed to convey morals, transfer traditions, and inspire the intellect when relating truth. Therefore, one can gain much from a story. The many morals to be learned from this story essentially describe how it is better to sacrifice this world's gain for the joy one will obtain by living a righteous life.

This story accounts the life of a determined man, a man who endured many odds, such as poverty, racism, and the devastation of death. This is the story of how a "simple man" can acquire in a single life works and words that are profound. How an "unassuming man" can influence others to stand out, and how an "uncomplicated man" can overcome the complexities of life.

This story seeks to emphasize "Godly morals," while laying out a practical strategy of how one may live a Christian life. In this story, at an early age a man became a husband, a father, and a Minister, disregarding the temptations of immorality: thus, proving God's way to be right, discrediting the traditions and rules of this devil's world, and has lived a ripe-old-age to tell it.

Preface

Although he missed much of this world's reward, "metrically speaking," this man's life still has balance: "medically speaking," his health has remained sound, concerning "family," he holds the respect of his wife and children, and in many communities, he has a reputation of being "righteous." His Church ministry spanned for over 52 years of service at the same congregation, and, at his 50th anniversary, the congregation hailed him as being *"a legend in his own time."*

This man has both learned and taught many lessons, and whatever he did in life he did with all of his heart, and did it well. He learned to farm, loved to cook, lived to fish and hunt, and "all-but" mastered most games he played, but nothing gave him more joy than preaching the word of God.

His quest to live a righteous life became his ultimate happiness, "bar none," and the delight he received while teaching others about "the righteousness of God" was a close second. Again, this man's life was not without problems, but he overcame them all through his faith in Christ Jesus. In short, this man's life was rich, because this man's life had purpose. This man truly believed God. This man became a Christian. This man's name was I.V. White, and *this, is his story...*

Written by George White, III

George White, III is an Evangelist for the Churches of Christ, and the third Son of I.V. White. He holds an A.S. degree in Business Management from Southwestern Christian College, a B.A. degree in Religion from Pepperdine University, a B.S degree in Human Services from Mercer University, and a Masters of Business Administration from the University of Phoenix. A proponent of Christian education, George White is a public speaker, an author, a debater, and a biblical instructor, who Ministers in Macon, Georgia where he resides with His wife, Mary, and their two teenage Sons, Giovanni, and George White, IV. He also has a daughter, Ola-Cymone White, who is currently away in college.

ACKNOWLEDGMENTS

FIRST AND FOREMOST, I THANK THE GOD OF heaven who is the head of my life, and who held me in the hollow of His hand through my troubled years, and allowed me to work in His vineyard for the last 53 years. I am thankful.

God knows the thoughts and intents of the heart. God knew before I was born into this world that in the year of 2011 I would be living at 233 Taylor Town Road in Abbeville, South Carolina and preaching for the Haigler Street Church of Christ. I thank God for the men who allowed me to stand on their shoulders so I could see with a spiritual eye. I'm thankful for all the people who touched my life in a positive way I thank the Haigler Street Church of Christ for allowing me to work with them for 51 years. Most of all, I thank God that He's not through with me yet.

THIS IS MY STORY

A special thank you goes to John Marshall who inspired me to tell my story. And helped me to put forth this book.

Introduction

IN THE BEGINNING

I T WAS IN THE YEAR OF 1957, WHILE WALKING DOWN the streets of Detroit, Michigan, as a salesman for the century mental craft corporation, selling waterless cookware, I spotted a large group of people sitting on a porch across the street. I saw an opportunity to make a sale. As I introduced myself and told them why I stopped by, they told me, have a seat and as soon as our bible study is over, we'll look at your goods.

The teacher was Ellis Bonner. He was a master teacher. He was saying, there's only one church in the bible. That sounded alright to me, I didn't know anything about the bible, and I thought he must be talking about the Baptist Church because to me, since I was a Baptist, everyone who was not a Baptist was religiously wrong. Then he said the Baptist Church is not in the bible. He further said John the Baptist not only never started the Baptist Church, but also was never a member of a Church. May I remind you that when I was 27 years old I could, and would knock a man down. He just went on and on about the Baptist being religiously wrong. It made me so angry I wanted to reach out and touch him right up side His head. But because I wanted to make a sale, I held my peace and didn't say a word.

After the class ended, they seem to be interested in my cookware if I could prove it would do what I said it would do. So I invited them all to my house for their next bible class. While they were having their bible class, I was preparing my food getting ready to demonstrate how to cook vegetable without using water. When I got through, they bought about a thousand dollars worth of cookware.

They invited my wife to go with them to the next bible study. Every Tuesday night they would come and take her to the bible study. One night she came home and she didn't get in bed, she just sat there, and after a little while she told me in a small voice, "I got baptized tonight." I asked, "You got what?" She said, "I got baptized tonight." I said, "What do you mean you got baptized tonight you already had one baptism." I was a little overbearing when I was a young man, and a little hard to get along with. She just knew I was going to raise the roof, she'd learn that Jesus was more important than her husband was. I didn't say too much. But she didn't know what I was thinking. I mean the very idea they had the nerve to come get my wife and baptize her and they didn't bother to ask me if it was alright. Sunday morning came she got up early put her best dress on, and looked at me tears almost falling and asked, "Will you take me to church this morning?" I really didn't want to take her but I had to. So I decided I wouldn't act like the devil, I put on my one suit, didn't have but one, and I went with her with a fully made up mind they will never get me.

The preacher stood up to preach and he started talking about this one church thing. I thought to myself, how in the world could this man be right when I knew about more than one church. He got right to the point. He hollowed out, "In Matthew 16:18 Jesus said, upon this rock I will build my church you see he said, Jesus has a church." Now they had schooled my wife and told her to write down all the scriptures, so I could read them when I got back home. He went to Ephesians chapter 4, verse 4. "There's one body and one spirit in the one body. The body is the church," he hollered and everyone said, "A-Men!" You know how it is with church members when you're preaching on something that they are not guilty of, they say *amen* real loud. He hollered, "Turn your bible to 1 Corinthians chapter 12 and verse 12 and 13. All of God's people are by one spirit baptized into the one body. Now then," he screamed, "what is the body?" The whole congregations hollered out, "The church!" "Turn your bibles to Ephesians chapter 1 verse 22" he said. "God gave Jesus the authority to be the head of His body and the body is the church."

It's amazing how man is a product of his teaching. When he's taught wrong in spiritual matters, he will believe the wrong thing, and this will cause him to obey the wrong thing, and become the wrong thing in the wrong place. I knew after one visit to the Church of Christ that I needed to make a change, but because they made me angry in the beginning I intended to show them that they would never get me. After about 6 months of going to worship service with my wife, I decided that I was hurting no one but myself, so I walked out in July of 1957 to be baptized into the body of Christ.

Just before I was baptized, Amanda Lyons of Abbeville, South Carolina came to Detroit, Michigan to visit her daughter, Julia Walker. R.N. Hogan, a gospel preacher, was conducting a gospel meeting at the Ford Avenue Church of Christ. Amanda Lyons was baptized at the age of 91 years old. She came back home being the only member of the Church of Christ in Abbeville, South Carolina. Gospel preachers, Alonzo Rose from Detroit, Michigan, John O. Williams from Toledo, Ohio, R. N. Hogan, from Los Angeles, California, J. S Winston from Cleveland, Ohio, Chester Vaughan from Camden, South Carolina, James Kennedy from Greenville, South Carolina and Richard Williams from Augusta, Georgia, got together and came to Abbeville, set up a tent on Branch Street, and begin preaching. They baptized about 30 precious souls. When the meeting was over they all had to go home and no one was left to preach and teach the church. So when I was baptized they were trying to find someone to go to Abbeville. After six months, I preached my first sermon. They were taking up money to build a meetinghouse and still trying to find a preacher that would go to Abbeville. I told the preacher, Alonzo Rose, that when my vacation comes up, I'm going to Abbeville and preach for them for two weeks. I didn't ask for a dime, I just went and preached for two weeks. When it was time for me to go back to Detroit, the old lady was just crying. She said, "Lord what are we going to do now?" I told her that I'd be back. I came back and told brother Rose, "I think I'll go to Abbeville and preach for them." Brother Rose said to me, "If you will go, the Ford Avenue Church would give you eighty dollars per month." With a promise of eighty dollars a month, I quit my job driving an eighteen-wheeler up and down the interstate making $500.00 per month. My wife quit her job, we gave away our furniture, put our clothing in the trunk of my car, and we came to Abbeville.

When we arrived in Abbeville, it was late at night. Sister Lyons was so happy she showed us where we were to sleep, and told us what we would have for breakfast. But we had all kinds of problems. We were accustomed to sleeping in a house that was warm at night as well as in the daytime. And here we are trying to sleep in a house that the wind blows right through. It was in October and we thought we were going to freeze to death. She had an old potbelly stove that she would get up in the morning and make a fire in, but when they went to bed at night the fire went out. I contracted the flu, I lost my voice and couldn't preach for three weeks. Thank God, I had an understanding wife who never complained. There were times we didn't have nothing to eat and Sister Lyons would go to the man she used to work for and borrow money to get us something to eat. My wife never complained. There was no need to talk about a job at that time because if you could get a job, it was doing yard work for some rich white man for fifty cent a day. The first year I was in Abbeville and with the help of God, we baptized fifty.

The first worship service in Abbeville was supposed to start at eleven o'clock in the morning. I made sure I set the right example by being in the building at 10:30 a.m. 11:00 a.m. came, no one was in the building but my wife, my one Son Emanuel, and me. Now there were only a few members at that time because not having a preacher, and it looked at the time they would not get one, they just went back to where they came from. Only nine women and some children remained, no men. 11:30 a.m., no members. 12:00 noon, no members. I began to think, what in the world did I quit my job for and my wife quit her job, and besides all that we gave away our furniture, to come to this God forsaken place to preach, and the members don't even come to worship service. I remembered what my mother told me when I came by her house on my way to Abbeville. When I told her, where I was going and why I was going, there she said to me, "You are the biggest fool I ever did see!" She said to me, "Those people don't have no money to pay you!" And she was as right as right can be because they didn't have no money to pay me.

But back to the worship service. About 1:00 p.m. one lady showed up. I asked, "Where is everybody?" She said, "They're coming, they had to cook their dinner. We are going to have dinner on the grounds today." Now at that time, I had no tolerance and no patience at all. I didn't know at that time that the only reason I was still alive was because God had put up with me for 27 years while I was doing everything but what He wanted me to do. I thought everything had to be corrected and it had to be corrected right then. So my first sermon was a fussing one. I mean I chewed them out for being late for worship service real good. I told them it's a sin to be late for worship service so that you can cook. No one was smiling about what I was saying, but they took it pretty good. They wanted a preacher so badly until they were willing to put up with me and my fussing. I never will forget the first collection. It was only $2.79 of which I had put in $2.00!

Chapter 1

pLaNtiNg My First CoNgregatioN

At that point, in my work in Abbeville, I wanted to go home and tell mama what I'd learn from God's word. Home was Madison, Georgia. I called daddy and asked him to get all his deacons and their wives together and have them at his house on Tuesday night at 8 o'clock. There was something they needed to know. Madison was about 100 miles from Abbeville. When I got to my daddy's house, they were all there. Three Baptist deacons, their wives, and a few friends. Daddy was the chairman of the deacon's board. Now remember I'd been preaching for about a year, so I'm still in the learning stage and I don't know how to explain the bible in an intelligent way. All I knew to teach was one church, how to get in it, and if you are not in it you are on your way to hell. They began to look at each other in a strange way, but they didn't say anything. At the end I asked, are there any questions? They had none. I told them I'd be back next Tuesday. The next Tuesday night the word had gotten around, that boy of George White is showing us some stuff in the bible we ain't never heard before, you need to be there Tuesday night--they were telling everyone. The next Tuesday night there were so many people there I could hardly get into the living room.

I started out with praying to get a religion. Fifty years ago, everyone in Morgan County claimed to have gotten a good religion. They would sing the Song, *I know I got religion yes, yes*. I turned to James chapter 1: 26-27 and asked someone who could read, to read it. I pointed out to them that God didn't command anyone to get a religion, and showed them that religion is not something you get in order to become a Christian. You practice pure religion, after you *become* a Christian by obeying the commands of the Lord. At that time, no one talked about a sinner's prayer, or being saved like the thief on the cross, or none of the other stuff dreamed up by man that you hear so much about today. Someone in the crowd suggested that since everyone wanted to hear, and since it was impossible to get into the house, that we should go down to the Masonic Hall where all could get in and hear. I told them that next Tuesday night we'd go to the hall.

The next Tuesday night there were so many people there they couldn't get into the hall. They didn't have air conditioning at that time, so all the windows were up and they were leaning in the windows to hear. The door was stopped up with people who were standing around the wall so no one else could get in. Someone in the crowd had called the Baptist preacher and had him sitting right up where I would be standing. I didn't know who he was so I thought he was someone who wanted to hear what I had to say. But he was there to prove that I was teaching false doctrine. Poor fellow, he didn't know that when a man is teaching what the bible teaches, you can't prove that he is wrong without proving that the bible is wrong.

I began by making the statement that the bible is the mind of God revealed to man. "Everything God wants us to know about salvation is in the bible. Everything God wants us to believe about salvation is in the bible. What we must do to be saved is in the bible. If what we believe and practice in religion can't be found in the bible, it's because God didn't say it, and therefore we need to stop believing it. He sat up and cleared his throat. I said praying to get a religion is not found in the bible, and everyone of you who prayed to get a religion and claim to have a good religion don't understand that no one can read in the bible where Christ, God, or the Holy Spirit ever commanded a sinner to pray. Every one of you who claim God saved you and then you got baptized because you were saved, made a religious mistake. If you want to be saved from all past sins, since Jesus is the Savior, since we depend on him to save us, why don't we just do what he told us to do, and do it like he said do it.

In other words, put first things first. Now let us look at what Jesus said we must do to be saved. Jesus said in Mark chapter 16 verses 15 and 16. He told His disciples to go into all the world and preach the gospel to every creature and he that believes--whoever it is that believes and is baptized shall be saved." I said you need to do it like Jesus said do it. I pointed out to them that there are some things that you have to follow instructions on or they will not work. I presented a parable to them. If a man buys himself a new car, the instructions say put water in the radiator, oil in the crankcase, and gas in the gas tank. Now you don't have to do it like the instruction say do it. But if you want it to run, you have to do it like the instruction say do it. If you don't believe that is true, then you should try putting water in the gas tank, put the oil in the radiator, and put the gas in the crankcase and see if you car will ever say a word.

"Jesus said he that believes: belief comes first, not praying. Baptism is the next step. *Shall be* is future tense. Jesus said *shall be* saved. All of you who thinks that you are already saved, I ask, how can that be? You are still living. When a man is baptized for the forgiveness of his sins, all he is saved from is his *past* sins. He is in a safe state, and if he remains in that state until he dies he will be, he *shall be* saved. :

All eyes were on the Baptist preacher. They expected him to say something. He just had to say something or lose all creditability. Then, his hand went up. He said, "all these people have already been baptized. Now if you can show me in the bible where anyone was baptized twice I'll eat this bible." He was holding up his bible. There were six high school students sitting around a table in the middle of the room. I had a little New Testament in my shirt pocket--I pull it out and asked, "Do you want to eat this little one or the big one?" I turned to Acts chapter 19:1 and handed it to one of those girls and told her to read. The other five girls got up and came around so they could also read along. They read where John had baptized twelve men and when they got to verse five they paused, I said, "Read it!" They continued and when they heard that *they were baptized*, all six of those girls looked at the Baptist preacher and said "ah", I said, "Read it all." He got up in a hurry and went out the door and he didn't come back.

About that time, the man who operated a dance hall pushed his way through the door. He said, "Brother White, these people out here want to hear too. This place is too small so come down to my place. I will sell no beer and I will unplug the record player." I told him I 'd be down to his place next Tuesday night.

The next Tuesday, they sent off to get another Baptist preacher who they had all the confidence in the world that he would shut me up. About three o'clock Tuesday evening the phone rang: it was mama. She said, "I called to tell you that Reverend Stentson will be here tonight and he said he's going to straighten you out." I began to shake in my boots a little bit. This was the man who was principal of the high school where I had went. He was so educated that he wore His hat in an educated way. I mean he never split a verb not even while joking. I got in my car and started to Madison, Georgia. On the way, my wife was upset with me about something I didn't do that I was supposed to do, so she was on my case. I said to her, "Now you know I've never debated anyone before, you need to pray for me." So we stopped the car and we prayed, then we continued on to Madison, Georgia.

When we got there, the place was full. The Baptist preacher had taken His seat up front. When I got up I said, "Tonight, I'm going to prove from the bible that the Baptist church doesn't belong to Jesus." When I made that statement, a man came through the door crying, tears just rolling down. He was ready to knock me down. He said, "You've insulted my mother." I said, " Where is she? I'll beg her pardon." He said, "She's dead and according to what you've said, she's in hell." Now my brother, my daddy, my mother, my sister, and my grandmamma were sitting up front. I saw grandmamma ease down beside the Coke machine and pick up a full bottle of Coke. I knew grandmamma was getting ready to crown him. I hollered, "Grandmamma put that bottle down!" That got his attention in a special way. I said, "If this man wants to hit me, I will not hit him back." At that statement, he turned and walked out and never came back.

So that you might be better able to understand where I'm coming from, I need to tell you that everyone in Madison, Georgia at that time prayed to get a religion, and when they said they had it, they had to tell their religious experience.

They had to tell why they know that God had given them a good religion. Then the church would vote to let them join the church. So I said, "There's nowhere in the bible where God, Christ, or the Holy Ghost ever commanded a sinner to pray and get a religion." I told them to turn their bibles to James chapter 1 verse 27. Now most of them didn't know where James was in the bible. So I had to send them to the table of contents to get the page number. When they all found the page, I had someone to read. I said, "You see, religion is not something to get, it's something you do after you become a Christian. Everyone looked at the professor, the Baptist preacher. He didn't say a word. I went on and on about everything the Baptists practice that's not according to the bible. Such things as voting people in, paying dues, calling the preacher reverend, and going to worship service just to entertain themselves with no thought at all about what pleases God isn't biblical." After every few minutes, I would stop and ask if there were any questions. The Baptist preacher didn't say a word. I give him credit though, because he was too educated to argue with facts. At the close of the lesson, I paused and asked one last time, "Are there any questions?" but he never said a word. One of His followers looked at him and asked, "Rev, you mean to tell me you don't have nothing to say?" He got up real slow, looked around and said, "Well this young man brought us the truth tonight and I want to recommend him to you," and he walked out. They got so angry with him that the church where he preached fired him.

The next Tuesday night the people had put so much pressure on the dance hall operator that we couldn't use his building anymore. The preachers and deacons of Morgan County had been busy all week encouraging people not to go and listen to that mess. That's what they called what I was teaching, mess. The crowd had thinned out. There was only about 25 or 30 people that showed up, and we went to a home where one of them lived.

But I could see that those that showed up were beginning to see the light. So for the first time at the close of the lesson I asked, "Don't you want to be a member of a church you can read about in the bible?" The answer from five of them was yes. I asked them to stand and give me their right hand. I asked each one of them, "Do you believe that Jesus Christ is the Son of God?" They said, "Yes." I explained that this confession caused Jesus to be put to death, but it will give you everlasting life after you put Jesus on in baptism. I was so happy. But this created a problem for me, because I had nowhere to baptize them. While I was calling and making arrangements, the devil got busy.

One man threatened to kill his wife if she got baptized. She backed out. The preachers and deacons got another one to back out. I was able to baptize only three of them. I had to drive to Atlanta, Georgia, seventy-five miles away to baptize them. I asked Lewis Guthrie, one of the deacons of the Simpson Street Church of Christ in Atlanta, Georgia to come down and have service each Sunday. He not only came himself, but many of the saints of the church came with him.

Planting My First Congregation

As soon as it had begun to get hot in June, I went to the school board and asked permission to put up a tent on school property. They said I could do it for $15.00 per week: I paid them and began looking for a tent. While looking for a tent, I was also calling Alonzo Rose, the minister of the Ford Avenue Church of Christ in Detroit, Michigan, the man who baptized me. I asked him to come and help me. I found a tent. The church where Brother Rose preached sent him and paid all his expenses. I wanted him to do the preaching and I would lead the singing. And you need to believe me when I tell you that when Alonzo Rose got in the pulpit, he could make it so plain a blind man could see it in the dark.

The First Night of the Meeting

That Sunday morning, Brother Rose got up and he preached a lesson that made everyone feel good. Everyone left saying what a preacher. What they were accustomed to from their preacher was not teaching, but a whole lot of moaning, screaming, and claiming that God told him to say and do all that stuff. The people would be crying and shouting, I mean jumping and running claiming the Holy Ghost made them do it. Their preacher would play on their emotions by talking about their dead mothers and how everyone would see them again in heaven. When Brother Rose got through everyone was happy but me. He knew what he was doing though, but I didn't. He was building up his crowd. I thought he needed to back up what I had told them which was that they needed to get out of that Baptist church. But Sunday night there wasn't an empty seat under the tent. Brother Rose got up and skillfully welcomed everyone there. Before he got into his planned lesson, he talked about the fact that the goal of every man should be heaven. God, he said, left it up to us to seek and find the narrow way, get on it and stay on it until death. Man is indeed a product of his teaching. Very few men are able to rise above their teaching. Therefore, if you teach a man wrong about religion, he will believe the wrong thing, causing him to obey the wrong thing and become the wrong thing in the wrong place.

Death in the Pot

I never will forget that Sunday night: he used as a subject, *Death in the Pot.* He went to 2 Kings chapter 4 verse 38-41 where Elisha the prophet came to Gilgal and found a dearth in the land, and the people were unable to grow food. The Sons of the Prophets were sitting before Elisha, hungry. Elisha instructed them to sit on the great pot and they were to cook up some pottage to eat. But someone in the crowd went into the field and gathered a lap full of wild gourds and while no one was looking, he chipped them up into the pot. When they began to eat, someone cried out, "There's death in the pot!" He pointed out that since they didn't have but one pot, they couldn't just throw it away. They had to add something to the pot that would take the poison out of the pot. From there Brother Rose went to work. He pointed out that the gospel of Christ is God's power on earth to save the lost (Romans 1:16). He also pointed out that there is only one gospel. "In Revelation 14:6 John wrote, *and I saw an angel flying in the midst of heaven, having the everlasting gospel to preach to them that live on earth*. But the gospel of Christ has been robbed of its saving power. While no one was paying attention, man added his opium to the gospel. He added his ideas to the gospel. He added his philosophy and what he thinks to the gospel." And he said, "The gospel mixed with all that man-made stuff is nothing but death in the pot. And in order to take the poison out of the gospel, we must add some faith in God's word. The bible teaches that we live spiritually by faith and not by sight. We've got to add some belief and trust in what God said. Jesus is the Savior of the world. He'll tell us what to do and how to do it so He can save us."

Chapter 2

THE CONVERSION OF MAMA

EVERY DAY I WOULD TALK TO MAMA ABOUT HER soul. She would listen so respectfully, and so quietly until I'd said all I knew to say, and then she would say, well, you got your faith and I got mine. Now this went on all week. Sunday morning she and her sister went to their church—the Baptist church. They came back and were in the kitchen cooking dinner. I was sitting in the living room listening to the two of them talk. They were talking about what happened at church that day. They had a custom that before the preacher got up to preach, they would have a prayer service. And they asked my mother and her sister to lead the prayer service and they had never prayed in public before, so they told them to get someone else. And when the preacher got up to preach, he preached on them. I listened real carefully to get all the details, and then I went into the kitchen with my bible. I turned to 1 Corinthians 14 verse 34 and then handed the bible to my mother to read. The verse said, *let your women keep silence in the churches, for it is not permitted unto them to speak.* Mama looked up at her sister and asked, do you think Reverend Laurence knows this is in the bible? I said to myself, "I've got you now."

Mama went down to the tent on Monday night. Brother Rose was shucking the corn and then grinding it up into meal. The man who told His wife he would kill her if she got into that *mess*, as he called it, was there each night. This time he said he would also kill himself. But every night when it was time to start, he would come up and sit on the last seat under the tent. He would have on dirty pants and shirt. Looking like he was so angry, he could bite a nail in two. I mean he was so mad that he could kill a rock. He did the same thing all week, sat on the last row and listened. Friday night we asked everyone to stand as they were invited to come to Jesus and give him their lives by believing in Jesus, repenting of past sins, confessing that they believe that Jesus Christ is the Son of God, and to obey the gospel of Christ by being baptized. Everyone stood. Mama came walking slowly down the aisle, behind her was daddy, grandma came next, and then my wife's mother came running up front. The lady whose husband was going to kill her got up and said, "I'm going to be baptized and I don't care what my husband does." When she got up to where I was, her husband jumped up and came towards me in a half trot. I didn't know what to do because I didn't know what he was going to do. But I didn't run. He got within six feet of me and raised His hand and said, "I couldn't hold out any longer."

On that Sunday morning, we were permitted to baptize in a man's fishpond. Many of the saints from the Simpson Street Church in Atlanta came down. They could sure enough sing. They were standing around the fishpond singing. *None but the righteous, none but the righteous shall see God.* And then they would say take me to the water, take me to the water, take me to the water to be baptized. I was happy yawl. I was waving my hands hollering, "Jesus will meet you in the water!" Twenty-two were baptized.

In the third week of the meeting, the deacons and preachers of the Baptist churches went to the sheriff and convinced him that he needed to make me take down the tent and leave town. Early Monday morning the sheriff came by. Mama was in the yard. He asked mama, is this where *that* preacher lives? She said yes sir. That was before you could yes and no to a white man in Madison, Georgia without getting knocked down. I had the window up so I heard him when he drove up. He said to her tell him to come out here. I went out. He asked, did you put that tent up down yonder? I said yes sir. He said, "Take it down." You are doing nothing but stealing church members, take it down. I said yes sir. I had better sense than to tell the sheriff of a Georgia city that I wasn't going to do what he *told* me to do. When he left, I got on the phone and call Brother Rose. I told him what had happened with the sheriff. He started fussing at me. He said to me, "White I told you to pay for that land and get a receipt." He told me that he knew as soon as the people began to leave those man-made churches they would try to run me out of town. I said to him I paid for the tent and I've got a receipt. He said, "You mean you've got a receipt?" I said yes. He said don't you take down that tent. So I didn't take it down. That night about time for service to start, here comes the sheriff. He pulls his car up beside the tent, rolled his window down and sat there while the service was going on. He did that for two nights and on the third night he called the man who was the spokesman for the group and said to him in a loud voice "these people are right you better join them!" and he went on back to town.

No one would rent us a place to worship, so we went to the undertaker shop and he let us use his tool shed to worship in. At that time in history, they didn't have professional gravediggers. They had picks and shovels the graves were dug by hand. He moved all his tools out for us. We called it Noah's Ark. When it rained, it rained in there just like it rained on the outside. We had an old potbelly stove put in there and that's where we started.

Now Alonzo Rose was a very popular preacher and he was known all over the brotherhood. He got busy raising money to build a building. But first, we had to get some land. The preachers and deacons convinced the people of the county that they shouldn't sell us any land and so no one would sell us any land.

We baptized an eighty-year-old lady, and she called one day and asked my mother to speak to me. I went to the phone and she said, "I hear tell that you are trying to find some land to build us a meetinghouse?" I said, "Yes, but we are having no luck." She said, "How would you like to build the church right up beside the highway?" I said, "I wish we could, but no one will sell us any land." She said, "I own that land and you can have it for one dollar." By this time Brother Rose had raised enough money to buy the materials we needed, the only thing left was to get a builder. Some contractors in Macon, Georgia heard about what we were trying to do. They were white, but they were Christians. They sent word that they would build the building for the cause of Christ and that it would cost us nothing. Early that Monday morning we went to the hardware store to buy some lumber, some blocks and cement—you know things we needed to get the foundation started. Now Madison, Georgia is a small city. You go through two red lights and you've just passed it. There was only one place in town that sold lumber. When we got there and told the man what we wanted he asked, "Are you all from that Church of Christ?" I said, " Yes sir." He said, "You will get no lumber here."

Earlier, some white Christians from the surrounding cities came to the meeting and came under the tent and sat down. But they just came to support what we were doing.

Those preachers and deacons in Madison, Georgia had convinced the storeowner that we were trying to integrate the church. Remember this was 1960 and they were not ready for integration.

Now my mother was the cook for the sheriff. Daddy said to the storeowner, "Call the sheriff." He did and the sheriff came. When the sheriff came into the building, he asked, "What's wrong?" Daddy spoke up. He said to the sheriff, "Tell this man we are not trying to integrate no church, we just want to build us a meetinghouse." The sheriff said, "Oh them niggers down there just mad because they stole so many of their members. Let them have whatever they want." Then the man began to give us stuff and at *no charge,* he gave us most of what we needed. I remembered Joseph when he said to His brothers who wanted to kill him and sold him into slavery he said, "To them *you meant it for evil, but God saw to it that it turned out for good."*

Elberton, Georgia was the next congregation planted with 23 baptisms. In 1970, a man named John Mills heard about my preaching and found out where I lived and came to visit me. He told me that he was supported by a group of white Christians who were interested in planting a church in all counties in Georgia that didn't have a congregation of the Lord's people. They asked would I do the preaching and I said yes. I would preach in Abbeville on Sunday and on Monday night, I would be preaching under a tent somewhere in Georgia. The white Christians would come in numbers and support the meeting. They did all the work, like setting up the tent, knocking on doors, and inviting people to the meeting. All I had to do was preach each night. They paid all my expenses.

My first work for them was in Eatonton, Georgia. This was my greatest experience. We had 60 baptisms in that meeting. And from there we went to Sparta, Georgia, 16 were baptized. From there we went to Sandersville, Georgia, 32 were baptized, and on to Greensboro, Georgia. From there we went to Fort Valley, Georgia. The church in Charleston, South Carolina called me to do the preaching under a tent on James Island, South Carolina when they decided to start a congregation of the Lord's people. There we had 22 baptisms. From there we went to Lake City, South Carolina to preach under a tent to try to get a congregation of the Lord's people started there, 23 were baptized.

I thank the God of heaven for allowing me to work in His vineyard for 53 years, and the good news is, He's not through with me yet. I'm still able at 81 years old to do gospel meetings and strengthen His church wherever I go. My voice is strong, I have no false teeth in my mouth, and my steps haven't shortened up yet. Thank God and praise His holy name.

Chapter 3

MY GREATEST

A S YOU CAN IMAGINE, DOING ALL THE YEARS I preached for the Haigler Street Church of Christ, there were many disapointing moments. there were many highs, but there were many lows also. some ups and some downs. there were times i didn't think i would make it another week. i will not attempt to adress all the disapointing things that happen along the way. listed below are a few things i believe deserves to be remembered. i choose to call them the greatest.

My Greatest Gospel Meeting

My greatest gospel meeting was conducted in Eatonton, Georgia, under a tent in 1970. We had a question box on one of the post in the tent. The Jehovah's Witness would come down during the day when no one was there and fill the box up with questions. The man who owned the radio station didn't like the Jehovah's Witness so he put me on the radio live each evening for two weeks, and I would answer their questions. 60 precious souls were baptized in that meeting. One night a son, his father, and his grandfather walked out to become baptized.

My Greatest Joy

My greatest joy was to teach and baptize a man who was an alcoholic. He could never get home from his job on payday with his money. His wife would meet him at the gate to get some money to buy food for the family to eat. After he was baptized, he put that bottle down, got himself a job, bought a house for his family, and sent his children to college. He was faithful to he Lord until his death.

My Greatest Shock

The greatest shock of my life came when I was in Terrell, Texas attending the Southwestern Christian College Lectureship. I had just checked into my hotel room when the phone rang. It was my son, George, calling. He said, "Daddy something bad has happened here." I said to myself, "What has those brethren done now?" I said, "What is it George?" He said, "Are you sitting down?" I said, "No". He said, "You better sit down." He told me that my 14-year old daughter, Berniece, was sitting in the chair and everyone thought she was just asleep, but she was dead.

My Greatest Disappointment

My greatest disappointment in my fifty-three years of preaching the gospel of Jesus Christ is that some of the men, whom I baptized and taught to become great teachers in the Lord's kingdom, allowed their love for me to turn into hate. They lied on me and said many evil things about me. But the Lord blessed me to have a forgiving spirit. I remember what Jesus said in Matthew chapter 5 and verse 11, "Blessed are you when men shall persecute you for righteousness". He said to rejoice and be exceedingly glad because this will make your reward in heaven great. It's shouting time when you are persecuted just because you are standing for the will of God, that is if you maintain the right spirit while being tested by the evil one.

My Greatest Sermon

The greatest sermon I ever preached was in Black Mountain, North Carolina in July 1985 at the Southeastern Youth Conference. 750 teenagers were in that place. I taught one lesson and 90 precious souls walked down the aisle. 60 repented and were restored to Jesus Christ while 30 were baptized into Jesus Christ.

The Devil's Greatest Job On Me

The greatest job the devil did on me was in Quincy, Mississippi. A white preacher from that town happened to be passing through Greensboro, Georgia where I was preaching under a tent. He saw the sign and stopped by. After services were over, he asked me if I would come to Mississippi and preach in Quincy, where he was the minister. He told me that there were no black Christians there. I asked him, "If we baptized some black people where would they worship?" He said, "They would worship where I preach." He got a tent and put it up. Two weeks before I was to go to Quincy, his church leaders fired him for inviting me to come. But no one told me anything about it. When I got down there, I couldn't find him, but the tent was up with a welcome sign in the yard. So I went under the tent that Sunday night prepared to preach. No one showed up. The Ku Klux Klan had warned everyone not to come under the tent. I stayed there for two weeks and not a single person came to the services. On the last night of the meeting one lady and a little boy came and she told me why no one came to the meeting. I had to pay all my expenses and travel back home disappointed. I had enough gas money to just get back home.

Chapter 4

A VESSEL OF GOD

(2 TIMOTHY 2:20)

TRULY, IT IS A BLESSING FOR ME TO BE HERE THIS morning, God has been so good to me. I just can't thank Him enough. He gave me Sons and daughters that I'm proud of, and some of the best friends in this world, and the best wife that a man could want. (How great it is) Giving honor to all those who are members of this great Church, and to those who might be visiting with us today, even those who have decided to become members later, I say good morning and thank God you are here.

My subject for today is a vessel of God (2 Timothy 2:20). When we think about a vessel, we think about a container, things that hold stuff that will be of service to the owner of the vessel. A vessel can hold many different commodities such as a cup can hold water, it can hold milk, it can hold coffee, it can hold orange juice it can hold whatever is put into it by the owner of the cup. Now the cup does not decide what goes into it, it is just a vessel to be used by its owner. The owner of the cup might decide to mix up a little orange juice and a little milk and a little coffee. The cup will say nothing for it's just a vessel to be used by the owner.

Figuratively speaking, a man or a woman is regarded as a container. A vessel if you please that is supposed to hold something put into it by the owner. The owner in this case is God. Those who belong to God are supposed to serve God. And use what God put in them to His glory and honor. But these men and women that belong to God are not like the cup, which has no mind of its own, and can't move until it is moved by its owner, and can't put anything into itself. Men and women that belong to God, have the ability, and the freedom, to set aside the wishes of God, in favor of their own wishes. They can set aside God's will for their will, and God's way of doing things for their way. You see like the cup, the man or the vessel can hold many different commodities. He can decide, he can make a choice as to what he will hold. He can hold good or he can hold evil: he can hold love or he can hold hate. He can hold his will or he can hold God's will. He can hold the Spirit of Christ or he can hold the spirit of

Satan. He can even try to mix it up, with a little bit of his will, and a little bit of God's will and a little bit of the devil's will, or a little bit of his wife's will. Paul said in 2 Tim 2:20 that in a great house there are many different vessels.

The great house that Paul is referring to here is the house that belongs to Christ. It is great because the Son of God built it, and God put His seal of ownership on it. This house was so great that the plans to build it were kept a secret by God for thousands of years.

But as time kept rolling, and the plans called for God's Son to build the house, God began to inform His people, that a change was coming. In Jeremiah 31:31 he said, *the days will come that I will make a new covenant with the house of Israel, and with the house of Judah, and it will not be like the one that I made with their fathers, when I took them by the hand and led them out of Egypt*. He then began to use Prophets to talk about a house that will be built in the future. In Isaiah 2:2, God told the prophet to tell His people that it shall come to past in the last days that the Lord's house shall be established in the top of the mountain, and shall be exalted up above the hills.

Everyone thought that this house would be a beautiful fantastic building. They could not know that God was talking about a spiritual house, because Peter said, in 1 Peter 1:10 that the Prophets inquired, and searched diligently for information about this house. Even the angels desired to look into the plan. But Paul tells us why they could not know. He said, in Ephesians 3:9 that from the beginning of time all this information was hid in the mind of God. The secret here, was not so much that a house was going to be built, but that only one house was going to be built, and that it would be a spiritual house, and God's Son would be the builder of it, and that it will belong to God's Son, Jesus and that salvation would be found nowhere but in this house. Now Paul said that in this great house there are many different vessels: some of gold, some of silver, some of wood, some of earth, some to honor, and some to dishonor.

I'm reminded of the parable found in Matthew 13:47. Jesus said that the church would be like a net, cast into the sea gathering some of every kind. And when the net was full, they came to shore and sat down and separated the good from the bad. Notice please, they didn't stop fishing and waste time separating the good from the bad until the fishing trip was over. So when the gospel net catches a bad fish, don't waste too much time trying to get rid of the bad fish, just keep on fishing. And when all fishing is over God will take care of the bad fish. And so it is in the church. The gospel of Christ, gathers some of all kind. Some gold, some silver, some wood, some earth, some to honor, and some to dishonor. All these different vessels are in the church. You see there are some great pretenders in the church. They are the people who don't act like themselves on Sunday. They act good, they look good, and they even smell good but only on Sunday. Old folks use to say, they are putting on a show. Some false teachers are in the church. Some liars are in the church. Some who commit adultery on a regular basis are

A Vessel of God

in the church, and we don't know who they are. We don't know the gold from the earth, or the silver from the wood. So we will have to wait until the judgment when God will send angels to clean up the church by separating the good from the bad, separating the real Christian from the counterfeit. Some will be gold, some will be silver, and they will love the Lord. They will be dedicated to the Lord, and His mission will become their mission, His work will become their work. The things he loves will become the things they love. And His home will become their home.

Now let us take a closer look at these vessels. They are all different; kind of like furniture in a house. Not all look alike. Not all serve the same purpose. Not all are made out of the same material. But all are in the house because the owner of the house, God, saw a need for them all. Allow me to compare your house to God's house. You see sometimes some stuff can be brought into your house that you don't want in your house, like a son who always comes in drunk. Or like my wife who always brings yard sale stuff into our house. I tell her you've got enough junk in this house already. But that don't help none. If you intend to go to heaven, sometimes you have to clean out your house.

And don't you know, that sometimes late at night church members are out acquiring some stuff. Oh, yes when the big jazz show comes to town some of our members will be scattered through the crowd, gathering and getting some of the devil's stuff. And they will bring that stuff into this great house. Because in this great house there are some vessels of gold, some vessels of silver, some wood vessels and some vessels of earth are in this house. God put them in here to serve Him. He does not expect these different vessels to have the same ability, the same talents, and be able to do the same things. Some of these vessels will dishonor the house by the things they do and say. While others will honor the house by the things they do and say. The important thing to remember here is, the honorable vessels must not allow themselves to be contaminated by the dishonorable vessels.

Don't allow yourself to be influenced by a dishonorable vessel to do and say wrong things. You see the vessels of earth are made of clay, and clay is weak and fragile. You have to be careful with it because if you drop it, it will break into pieces. Now it is the job of someone to help the clay become silver and gold because you do have in this great house some vessels of clay. You have to be so careful with them, you have to be careful of what you say to them, for they will get offended at the dropping of your hat. And they will stop giving, and they will try to get everyone else to stop giving too. They will leave the church, and they will try to get everyone else to leave also. They do all of this because they are weak and fragile. And then, there is the vessel of wood. Wood can easily catch on fire in the house, and if you don't put it out, it will burn the house down. No preacher should have to spend all of His time putting out fires in this great house. And sometimes when he puts one fire almost out, there's a group of unholy gossipers starting another fire. And before he can get this one all the way under control, there is a little clique sitting in the back of the house, finding fault of every word that's said: grumbling and complaining to start another fire. And before he can get this one under control there's another fire getting started by the brethren who supposed to be helping the preacher, but instead of helping, they are contending with him for power. They want to know who has the power to tell whom to do what. In Matthew 28:18 Jesus said all power in heaven and on earth belongs to me. So you can see who has the power. THEY SAY WE ARE ALL EQUAL. Now everyone knows that the bible does not teach that everyone in the church is equal. In Matthew 25:14 notice please that they were not all given the same amount, but the were all given all they could handle. Reminds me of Miriam and Aaron, the brother and sister of Moses. In Numbers 12:1-11 they thought that they were equal to Moses. Listen to them, they didn't like the woman Moses married. And when people don't like you for any reason, they have a desire to do something to you. They said, we are just as good as Moses is, didn't God speak to us also? The bible says God heard them. Now we know that God hears everything. But when He heard this it caused Him to pay special attention to these two misguided souls. And to make sure they understood, God called all three of them to come out here. And then he told Miriam and Aaron come a little closer, to step forward. God asked them, you mean to tell me that you were not afraid to speak against my servant Moses, and Miriam turned white as snow. And Moses had to beg God to forgive them. Church members need to be reminded that when they get upset and start gossiping about the elders or the preacher that God is listening. Now Jesus has all power, but He gave some power to the preacher, and some to the elders. And where there are no elders, the preacher is the only one in the congregation with the power to set in order, everything that's out of order (Titus 1:5: 2 Timothy 4:1-2).

Remember now, that God didn't put leading brethren in the house, they are not in the book. He didn't put trustees in the house, and they also are not in the book. Church members should not be starting fires in the house because you know that when a fire breaks out, it requires all your attention. Everything else has to wait until you get the fire out. You have no time for anything else until the fire is out. You don't even think about a bible class in someone's home, until the fire is out. The reason why some congregations never grow is because they have too much wood and clay in them. And when a good preacher goes there, and takes God's word and tries to transform the clay into silver and gold, the clay breaks into pieces, and the wood catches on fire, and all the preacher can do is try to get out alive. These are vessels of wood. If you are a vessel of clay and wood, you need to allow the transforming power of the blood of Christ to transform you into a vessel of silver and gold. You don't get all discourage because you can't perform like someone else. Look at a glass made of fine crystal and a plan old jelly glass, you can drink just as much milk out of the jelly glass as you can drink from the glass made of fine crystal. Makes no difference whether you are gold or silver. Wood or earth, you found your way into the house, and you should be trying to do a job for God. God put you in this great house to do a job for him. Now all these vessels were dirty at one time because all were in sin at one time or the other. They had to be cleaned up. They allowed the blood of Jesus to clean them up, and God put them in the house, and they became vessels to be used in the house (underscore the word *used*). We should rather wear out in the service of God than to rust out sitting and doing nothing. God expects us to grow into vessels of gold and silver, and He expects us to stay clean, because he can't use no dirty vessels. However, he knew that no vessel could be used continually without getting a little dirt on them every now and then, even if by accident. So he put a plan in place. Just like when your cup gets dirty, you fix some dishwater, put some dish washing liquid in the water, get yourself a washing cloth, and you wash your cup. The big difference here is, you put the cup in the water, the cup couldn't resist. The cup didn't say anything. But you can't bring God's vessels to the cleansing power of the blood of Jesus, these vessels have a mind, they have to want to come. They can think and make decisions and sometimes they make a decision not to come, but the cleansing blood of Jesus that cleanses us from all of our sins is available. The only thing that stands between a dirty vessel and a clean vessel is repentance.

Now since there is a judgment coming, and since Peter said it will start at the house of God, it will start with the vessels that belong to God. We'd better get ourselves cleaned up. And we'd better stay clean, because when the end does come, God will send some angels to this great house to separate the dirty from the clean. In Matthew 13:49 Jesus said when the end come, he will send forth His angels to separate the good from the bad, the evil from the wicked, the clean vessels from the dirty ones. What a time it will be in that great getting up morning. When the trumpet sounds and the graves give up their victims, and all the clean vessels get up, and all the clean vessels that still live be changed and they go up to meet the Lord in the air, so he can take them to that great family reunion in the sky. What a time it will be, when the saints go marching in. John said it will be a number that human beings can't number: and I want to be somewhere in that number when the saints go marching in. I've got to stay clean, because I want to be in that number when the saints go marching in. And if I make a mistake I want to hurry and get cleaned up again so that I can be in that number when the saints go marching.

Chapter 5

BE SURE YOUR SINS FIND YOU OUT

1 JOHN 3:4 SAYS, "WHOSOEVER COMMITS SIN, transgresses also the law. For sin is the transgression of the law of God." When we talk about sin, we are talking about failing to do what God commanded us to do, or doing those things that we are commanded not to do. The Greek word for sin is *missing the mark*. It matters not how close you come to hitting the target, if you missed it, you didn't hit it. So you missed the mark. There is no room in God's program for us to be almost right or almost wrong. It's either right or wrong. Paul recorded it this way, in Romans 3:23 he said, all

have sinned and come short of the glory of God. So then, sin is coming short of what God commanded. And it cheats us out of our heavenly reward.

Whoever breaks God's law, commits sin. God gave His people a law to regulate their conduct. Whenever we depart from God's law, we find ourselves in sin. And God's law determines what's right and what's wrong in all cases. When we fail to do what God's law demands of us, we've broken the law of God, because sin is breaking God's law. When we do those things that God's law forbids, we've broken God's law, because sin is breaking God's law (1 John 3:4).

Today, I want us to look at a scripture found in Numbers chapter 32:20-23. I want to use as a subject, *Be Sure Your Sins Will Find You Out.* By way of introduction, Ruben and Gad pledged the men in their group to fight on the other side of Jordan for Israel, and not return until they conquered the land. Moses agreed to this arrangement, and promised to let them have the east side of the river if they were willing to do this. But he warned them about keeping their word. He said to them, keep your promise. If you deviate from this procedure, remember the dogs of retribution are on your trail. You will not get away with it, your own sins will find you out.

This problem called sin is a difficult one. Because lodged within the bosom of all of us lies the raw material for the commission of any kind of sin. That's the meaning of the passage in James 2:10. James says if you offend or break the law in one point, you have broken the whole law. This does not mean that if you commit one kind of sin, you might as well commit all the others: it means if you commit any sin, you have within you the power to commit every sin. Each one of us has within us the power to sin. So don't boast about your moral insulation. Don't brag about the fact that you are a good Christian. Don't brag about what you will never do. Thank God, that he kept the pressure off of you. You were never in a situation where you had one second to decide whether you will shoot a man, or let the man shoot you.

All sin can cause much heartache and pain. Not only to ourselves, but to the people who love us, it causes heartache to the people who work with us, it causes heartache to the people who worship with us, and even the people we love. Tears and sorrow follows in the path of the transgressor. As Proverbs 13:15 reads the way of the transgressor is hard. And there are many kinds of sins.

There are moral sins, sins of the flesh: sins of sexual immorality. God ordained marriage and that's the only cure for sexual sins. I've heard men say, "I don't need a wife", But if you don't need a wife, then you don't need a girlfriend. You don't need to be courting. If you need to be courting, you need a wife.

There are temperamental sins, sins of the disposition. Where people are hard to get along with, they have a bad attitude about everything. And it's their way or no way.

There are ethical sins, sins that deal with dishonesty and discourtesy. Some people can't even play a game without trying to cheat. They are dishonest people.

There are spiritual sins, sins that deal with indifference, and the neglect of spiritual things. Being a part time Christian in God's full time church is a sin.

There are domestic sins, sins that deal with a nagging wife and a misunderstanding, mean, hard to get along with husband and children who talk back and disrespect their parents. There's the sin of pride, where we over estimate ourselves, and think ourselves to be better than we really are. There are social sins, sins of prejudice against races and religion. There is the sin of rebellion where we rebel against governments, we rebel against law enforcement, and we rebel against church leadership. And we even shake our fist against God, and rebel against him.

There's the sin of gossiping, where we talk about other people, saying things about them that are not true. Trying to make folks believe that it is true. Allowing our mouths to destroy someone's character and kill the influence of some good people. Then there's the sin of killing little spiritual babies. You know how when you baptize a man or woman, they become a spiritual baby in Christ. And they need to be fed on milk. The only thing that a baby can eat when they first come into this world is milk. And you've got people in the church who instead of feeding them spiritual food, which is the sincere milk of the word. They will take them aside and start feeding them garbage. And kill them as dead as last year's newspaper. You know take them aside and begin telling them what is wrong with the leadership. What is wrong with sister so and so? And you know they can't stand that stuff. All they can stand is the sincere milk of the word. But don't ever forget that your sins will find you out it's just matter of time. The only thing that stands between the sinner and the judgment is time.

Sin will find you out in your body. The body is the battleground, the field upon which the soul fights its battle with wrongdoing. If sin wins, the body pays the price. Sin will find you out in your character. It will destroy the cords of moral strength and weaken you for future trials. Sin will find you out in your children. By the force of your example, they will imitate you, and find themselves in the same boat with you. Sin will find you out in your conscience. The fear of being caught, will make your sleep run away from you at night.

You know sin is like buying things on credit, it is easy to get but hard to pay back. Sin will take you farther than you intended to go, it will keep you longer than you intended to stay, and will cost you more than you want to pay. Knowing all of this, you worry about the consequences, the price you will have to pay if you get caught. And you will get caught. If you don't get caught by man, God saw you and got you recorded in His book.

Be sure your sins will find you out. This statement is not true because it's in the bible, but it's in the bible because it's true. The skeletons will not stay in the closet. They will kick the door down and get out when you least expect them. They will show up in the living room when you are having company and reveal themselves to your guests. They will even walk downtown and tell everyone they meet where they came from.

The vindication of this passage walks the streets of every American city. I know it's true that your sins will find you out. Ask the drunkard whose body has been destroyed by liquor, and whose mind has been rendered inefficient by drugs, and he will tell you that your sins will find you out. Ask the cheating partner in a marriage, whose broken home testifies to the cheap results of playing with sin and he will tell you that your sins will find you out. Ask the drug dealers who lived in a mansion, (notice I said *lived* past tense) drove the most expensive cars, and had money in more than one bank, but the law caught up with him, and took His mansion, took his cars, and his money and put him in jail.

Ask God about it and He will tell you whatsoever a man sows that shall he reap. Ask God about it and He will tell you in Luke12:3 what you speak in the dark will be heard in the light. Sin is always self-deceiving. Watch the woman who brags about the fact that we've been married for 50 odd years and we've never had a cross word. Everyone knows she's a lying woman. Watch the man who is always bragging about how he loves his wife. The very fact that he feels like he has to convince you that he loves his wife tells you, he's an abusive husband.

Sin is always anti-common sense. Common sense will tell you that if drugs will destroy one man's life, it will do the same thing to you. But sin is anti common sense. You think you are smart enough to figure out a way to use drugs and not get addicted. Common sense says that if liquor will make a man act like a fool, talk like a fool, walk like a fool and even look like a fool, and will destroy his body, it will do the same thing to you. But sin is anti-common sense. Even judges who know how many men they have had to put in jail because of what whiskey made them do, drink themselves, because sin is anti-common sense.

The bible talks about a boy who had a good father, and lived in a good home but he decided to leave. We call him the prodigal son. Didn't make no sense for him to leave, but sin is always anti-common sense. And the bible says that he found himself one day feeding hogs, and was so hungry he wanted to eat what the hogs were eating. But he came to himself. Which seem to indicate, that up to this time he was in a state of temporary insanity. Any sensible man will not lose His soul over some stuff he knows he will have to leave behind when he leaves this world. But millions today love the things that God made, more than they love the God that made the things. Common sense says if I want a happy home, I must create an environment in my home that makes for peace and happiness. I must not be mean, hard to get alone with, contrary to everything my wife wants, and insist on having my way all the time, until I run my wife off, and then cry because she is gone. Sin is anti-common sense. Some people who think themselves to be so smart, do some of the dumbest things you ever seen a man do.

Common sense says if I want to be saved, it just makes good sense to listen to the man who has the power to save me, that's Jesus. I need to remember that Jesus is the Savior and He knows what I need to do so He can save me. It makes no sense to be talking about what reverend so and so said when it comes to salvation. I need to listen to Jesus who is the Savior. But sin is anti-common sense. That's why when a man starts looking for salvation, he starts looking for the church of his choice. He makes a big mistake, but sin is anti-common sense. He tells himself that one church is as good as another, because sin is anti-common sense. He's looking for a church with large choirs, and professionally train musicians that can play real good. That makes him feel good you see. He only goes to worship so he can be made to feel good. He never thinks about what makes God feels good. Common sense says if Jesus had to die, shed His blood to build the church he owns, no other church is as good as that one. But sin is anti-common sense.

Oftentimes people justify their misconduct by appealing to the majority rule. They say, 'everyone is doing it'. Let me tell you something, the worst reason in the world to do anything is because someone else is doing it. The fact of the matter is not everyone is doing it. And if everyone were doing it, that still wouldn't make it right.

Others think that they know how far to go in sin. They pride themselves in being moderate and temperate in all things. They say it's all right to drink a little, as long as you don't get drunk. But you can't regulate sin. Sin has a way of dictating to the transgressor. Sin is never satisfied until it reaches it culmination. In James, we are told that sin, when it is finish, brings forth death. And you can rest assured that sin will not stop short of its goal. On the other hand, being moderate is not commendable if you are moderate about things that are wrong.

We would never recommend being a moderate killer. We wouldn't say it's all right to steal every now and then. If a thing is wrong, it shouldn't be done at all, because there is no right way to do a wrong thing. Many fail to realize that the master strategy of the devil, is to get you started on a low level and then increase you to a high level. Your sins will find you out.

You know what they say. You can fool some of the people some of the time, but you can't fool all the people at no time. Sin has a way of becoming a part of you. The first time you do what you know is a sin it will bother you. You'll think about it when you get in the bed at night. But the next time, it won't be quite as bad. And after a while, it will become a habit and you'll begin to look forward to the next time. And you know how hard it is to break a habit.

It is said that a rich man lost a real expensive diamond on the beach. He had intended to have it put in his ring but on this day, he had it in his pocket. Somehow he lost it on the beach. A beggar came by while the man was looking for His diamond and asked him for a dime. He thought to himself I have plenty money. I can just go and buy myself another diamond. So he said to the beggar, I lost a very expensive stone somewhere on this beach, and if you find it you can have it. So the beggar came up with what he thought to be a foolproof plan. Every stone he would pick up that was not the diamond he would throw it in the ocean. So he wouldn't have to pick that one up again. Every day he would get on His knees and start picking up stones and throwing them in the ocean. He got into a habit of picking up stones and throwing them in the ocean. Finally, one day he picked up the diamond. He was so happy. His plan worked. Now he can go buy himself some of the things he so badly needs. But because he had gotten into a habit of throwing stones into the ocean, before he knew it, he had thrown it in the ocean. Whenever you get to a point where you can commit a certain sin as easily as throwing a stone in the ocean, sin is in control of your life.

There is something about wrongdoing that demands continuance. You may say I will do it just this one time and then I'll quit. That is usually not the case. The sin you commit is a seed sown, and though you may not plant any more seeds, the one already planted in your personality will come up and bring forth fruit. For one thing, the person thinks he's getting by with his sin because he doesn't have to pay for it immediately. And when he gets by so long, he thinks he can get by forever. No wonder Ecclesiastes 8:11 say, because sentence against an evil work is not executed speedily or because the punishment does not come immediately, the man thinks he's getting away with it and he will keep on doing it. But your sins will find you out because you cannot apply the brakes whenever you want to. And one of these days, that sin will become a part of you as much as your nose is a part of your face.

So let me plead with you to remember that sin has an intelligence of its own. It will find you out. But in spite of all I've said, the gospel of Christ has a remedy for our sins. And since you can't un-say what you've said that was wrong, you can't undo what you've done that was wrong, and you can't go back to do what you fail to do when you found out what you needed to do for God. You need to turn to Jesus this morning for your salvation. He's so good, a Savior who is full of grace and mercy.

The cross of Christ is God's answer to the cleverness and deadliness of sin. It's the only answer. So if you are struggling this morning with sin, you need to know that we are not left in despair. Jesus is the answer for your sin problem. The blood of Christ will cleanse us from all sins. He said a long time ago through the Prophets, *though your sins be as scarlet they shall be white as snow*. God will forgive you and give you the power to win, he only asks for your consent, so he can do in you what you cannot do for yourself.

God has made ample provisions for your spiritual needs, and has brought you through many dangerous situations. Thank God this morning that he allowed you to be here this morning with another chance to let Him fix up what you messed up. Let Him take your feet out of the sinking sand, and place them on the narrow way. All he wants is your consent. As David said long ago in Psalms 73:2, "*My feet were almost gone, and my steps had almost slipped.*" For many of us, God took control of our lives just in time. Because we had the devil's hook in our mouth, and he was reeling us in, and we were not even trying to get off the hook. Some are in that same situation this morning. The devil is slowly but surely reeling you in. But thanks be to Jesus this morning that came to rescue the lost. God wants to save you this morning and all He wants is your consent. He said a long time ago, *behold I stand at the door of your heart and knock.* All He wants is your consent. *"Come unto me,"* He said, *"and I will give you rest."* Let me say it again. All He wants is your consent.

Your sins are too much for you. You are no match for the strategy of the devil. Realize this, and turn your eyes upon Jesus. He has the answer for your sin problem. He will forgive the past, and give you power for the future. "Will you come to Him this morning?"

Chapter 6

BUILDING FOR ETERNITY

(MATTHEW 24:1-8 MATTHEW 25:1-13)

God made an appointment for all of us with death. And He will see to it that we keep that appointment. We know that when death comes for us God will usher us out of this world into eternity, to await the judgment. Knowing this, since we've set heaven as our goal, and since we don't know how much time we have left to reach our goal, pressing upon our minds should be the fact that we need to get busy now getting ready to go to our eternal home—preparing ourselves to live happy in eternity.

All men are subject to the restrictions and privilege of time and because of this, learning to use time wisely and correctly is a most important need since we don't have long to stay here. Job said in Job 14:1, man that is born of a woman is of a few days, and they are full of trouble. Moses said it all when he said in the 90th chapter of Psalms we spend our lives as a tale that's told. He said, Lord teach us to number our days. If you've lived to be 37 years old chances are real good that one-half of your life is already gone. If you've lived to be 47 years old chances are good that two-thirds of your life has already been spent. And if you've lived to be 75 years old, you've spent 25 years asleep. Proving that you don't have always to get prepared to meet death. It is said that a small boy was taken to church by his grandfather and he heard the preacher preach about eternity. He was so impressed, that when he got home it was still on his mind. He asked his daddy, how long is eternity? The old man said to him son, suppose we load up a ship with 100 thousand tons of sand, and every 100 thousand years throw out one grain of sand. How long do you think it would take us to unload the ship? There was no answer but the little fellow got the point that eternity has a beginning and no ending.

The word eternal means without ending. It means everlasting. It means to us, the duration of time after death, it means to live in a place not controlled by time, it means everlasting. So to build for eternity means to build up a store house of things that will last forever with God, in a place that will last forever with God. Now you've got to make sure that when you leave this world you go to the right place. There's more than one place to spend eternity in. Now, I will admit that this is not the easiest thing in the world to do. Sacrifices will have to be made by everyone who intends to spend eternity with God. We have to do some things we may not want to do. We have to go sometimes when we don't feel like going. We can't be like the creeks and rivers running around everything that gets in our way, and always running down hill. We even have to do some things that are hard for us to do. Sometime we have to run up hill, against the wind. But those of us who intend to spend eternity with God, know that Jesus said in John 14:2, *"I'm going"* he said, talking to His disciples, *"to prepare a place for you"*, and we know that it takes prepared people to live in a prepared place. So we need to hurry and get ourselves ready to live in eternity with God.

There are many who are good at getting gain in this world. They believe that the most important thing in life is getting some more money, so that they can buy some more things. They believe that if they can get their hands on enough money they will be forever happy. At that point, money becomes their God. Now it's not a sin to have money and it's not a sin to have a whole lot of money. But if you get your money the wrong way, and if you spend your money on the wrong things, and if you love your money more than you love God, your money will become your God and that will allow your money to send you to the wrong place in eternity.

Let us listen to what the Holy Spirit said to Paul. God had this recorded for our good. In 1 Timothy 6:9, he said, *"They that would be rich, those who make their supreme goal getting some more money, will fall into temptation and a snare, they fall into many foolish and hurtful lusts, which drown men in destruction."* Notice please, He didn't say those that are rich, but those that would be rich, those that are trying to get rich, those that spend their time wishing they were rich, yes those that love money more than they love God. Some will do anything to get some money. The only reason why a man will beat His friends out of their money is because money is his god. The only reason why a man will cheat, lie and do wrong things to get money is because money in his god. The only reason why a man will rob God is because he loves money more that he loves God. Paul said that the man that spends all of his time trying to store up money, will fall into temptations and a snare. While you are trying to store up all the money you can get, you will err from the truth.

The question needs to be asked by everyone is, what will I take with me as I go into eternity? First, let me talk about some things we will not take with us when we go. You will not take your money. You may be a millionaire today, but if you die tonight, someone else will be a millionaire tomorrow. We brought nothing into this world and it is a sure thing we will carry nothing out. Don't get too attached to your things because when you go, they stay. And no one should lose their soul over something they have to leave behind when they go. By the way, you don't own anything anyway. The cattle of a thousand hills belong to God, and all the silver and gold in this world belongs to God. Even those few pennies you have in your pocket belong to God. God allows us to use these things while we live. He puts them in our charge, we are stewards over these things, and we can decide how they will be used. However, we should never forget that one day we will stand before God and give an accounting to Him as to how we used those things He gave us to manage for Him. So be careful what you do with what God put in your hands to manage for Him. If you use them wrongly, they will send you to the wrong place in eternity. God gave you your life, don't live it wrongly. God gave you your talent don't use it wrongly. Don't use your influence wrongly. If you do, it will come up again in the judgment. Whatever you are blessed to have, use it in a way so God can be glorified.

You can't take popularity with you when you go. Some folks will do anything to be popular. But being popular with man does not impress God at all. You need to be real. Don't put on and pretend. Just be who you are. If you are not what God want you to be, don't pretend to be, change. As the old folk use to say, "JUST BE WHAT YOU IS, AND DON'T TRY TO BE WHAT YOU AIN'T. BECAUSE IF YOU TRY TO BE WHAT YOU AIN'T, YOU AIN'T WHAT YOU IS." The reason why some people will never know what they need to know is because they pretend to know what they don't know. No man knows everything. So if you don't know all you need to know, just ask someone who knows, and keep marching up the King's highway. You should not allow nothing or no one to take the place of God in your life. Mark 12:30 tells us *to love the Lord your God with all your heart.*

There are some things that will go with you into eternity. Romans 2:16 says God shall judge every secret of man in that day by Jesus Christ. So then, as you stand before God in the judgment, all the wrong secret things you did, and didn't repent of will be in the judgment with you. So you had better be careful about all that stuff you have to keep under cover. There is a secular song that says, if walls could talk what a story they could tell. Now you and I know that walls don't have to talk for God to know what is said and done behind closed doors.

Your words will be there. Matthew 12:36 tells us that *every idle word that men shall speak shall be brought into the judgment.* You've got to be careful about what you say. Let me ask you something. Would it be all right for us to have a video of everything you've done and said during the past week and we play it before this audience? Think about it: but remember, God heard you, and God saw you. Therefore, God put it on your record, and it will be there until you allow God to take it off by being forgiven. 2 Corinthians 5:10 tells us that all the deeds we've done God knows about them and that every man will have to stand before the judgment seat of Christ to be rewarded according to His deeds, whether they be good or bad. In Revelations 20:12 John said, "*I saw the dead small and great stand before God… the books were opened.*" Now, God don't need no book. He knows what you've done. Some time we do stuff, and we don't repent of it: and after 20 or 30 years we've forgot about it. God is going to bring out the record to refresh our memory—to make sure we know that he's not mistreating us when He says, *"Depart from me."*

Open up your bibles to Matthew 25:1. This is where I've been trying to get from the beginning. Jesus presents a parable. A parable is a lesson taught on things we know about to help us understand spiritual things we don't understand. This parable is about a wedding that takes place. It is compared to the coming of Jesus, when the end comes. Jesus said *then*. Then is an adverb of time, meaning when. Then *when* the end comes. Now the bible was divided up into chapters and verses by man. The 25th chapter of Matthew is a continuation of chapter 24. When he was asked when will the end come? Jesus said *then* when the end comes, the kingdom will be like ten virgins who took their lamps and went forth to meet the bridegroom, five were wise, and five were foolish.

The kingdom here is the church, the bridegroom is Jesus, and the wise and foolish virgins represent you and me. What Jesus is saying is when the end comes, the church will be like these ten virgins. Some will be wise some will be foolish. Who are the wise? The wise are those who get prepared for what they know will come. Like a man who buys himself a casket, he knows he will need it one day. He buys it before he needs it, because when he needs it he can't buy it. However, who are the wise? Matthew 7:24 reads *whosoever hears these saying of mine, and does them shall be like a wise man who build his house on a rock.* And everything hit it. The rain, the floods, and the wind, but the house didn't fall, because it had the right foundation. So the wise are those who hear what Jesus said and believes it and does it. The wise are those who build their life on a good foundation, the foundation of Jesus Christ. They know that the storms of life will come, and shake their foundation, but if their life is built on Jesus Christ.

When the storms of mistreatment hit you, Jesus will be standing with you. When the storms of sickness hit you, Jesus will stand by you. Then after a while, when death comes, the soul will be in good shape to live with Him in eternity.

Who are the foolish? *Whosoever hear these saying of mine and does them not, shall be like a foolish man who built his house upon sand.* I know of no one who is dumb enough to work hard, save his money and then build his dream house upon sand. Notice, Jesus said the man who hears and will not do, is just as foolish as a man who will build his house on sand.

Now these virgins all were suppose to meet the bridegroom. They all had the same chance and the same amount of time to get ready. The difference between the virgins was, the wise were prepared for a long wait. They had oil in their lamps, and they had extra oil in their vessels.

The foolish had lamps just like the wise, they had oil in their lamps but they didn't have any extra, even though they did have time to get some. There are many today, if they could have died when they were first baptized they would have been saved. But since the time when they were first baptized, the oil in their lamps have long ago run out, and they are not trying to refill their lamps. Thank God, you still have time to refill your lamp. Don't be like the foolish virgins and wait too late.

And while the bridegroom tarried they all slumbered and slept. The bridegroom is Jesus. He is tarrying in heaven now, waiting for the time when God shall charge the angels to sound the trumpet, telling everyone that time shall be no more. While He is tarrying, we should be storing up oil in our vessel. The oil represents righteousness. Righteousness is not something you can loan or borrow because no man has any to spare. With all you've got, you need, because it is just barely enough to make it in with none to spare. You know what Peter said in 1 Peter 4:17. He said, judgment must begin at the house of God. Peter said *if*, the righteous will scarcely be saved. The righteous will make it in with none to spare. It makes no difference how much righteousness you have, you'll have barely enough to make it in. You know the bible teaches us that he that has more, more is expected of him. You will not even have enough to loan your children any. They must build up their own righteousness.

How do you build up righteousness? You build up righteousness by doing right. In 1 John 3:7 John wrote, *"Little children let no man deceive you. He that does right is righteous, just like Christ is righteous."* Sinning, is just like buying stuff on credit, it easy to get, but hard to pay back. Don't be deceived, no man can live in sin and die righteous. You can't live wrong and die right. Listening to Jesus and then do what He said do, is just the right thing to do.

At midnight a cry was made. Behold the bridegroom is coming, go out to meet Him. *At midnight*, a time when everyone should be asleep, and that tells me that it's going to be a surprise to everyone. 2 Peter 3:10 says, *"The day of the Lord will come as a thief in the night."* It will be a surprise, just like the wedding of long ago. The bride didn't know when the groom was coming to get her. So she wanted to be ready when he came. Therefore, she would place hearers along the road that the groom had to travel to let her know He's on His way.

That's the way it's going be when Jesus comes back to get the church. We don't know when He will come, but we do know He's coming, and we need to be ready. Because one day, just as sure as I'm standing here, the Lord will come down from heaven, and an angel will be sounding a trumpet, proclaiming with a loud voice, Jesus is coming to get His bride. When that trumpet start sounding off what a time it will be. Can't you see it? PAINT A PICTURE IN YOUR MIND. A man draws back his hand to slap his wife, and the trumpet sounds: he stays his hand. Some will be raising his or her glass to take another sip of old granddaddy, and the trumpet sounds and he puts down the glass. Some will be pulling off their clothing to get in bed with a strange man or woman, and the trumpet sounds and they will put their clothes back on real fast, hoping that the Lord didn't see them. Some will be breaking and entering someone else's house. Can't you see him, he just picked up a TV set and the trumpet sounds and he drops it on His feet. Some will be telling someone off, and the trumpet sounds and they hurry to say I'm sorry.

As I told you before Jesus is the bridegroom and the Church of Christ is the bride. And one of these days Jesus will come back to get His bride. All eyes will see Him. 1 Thessalonians 4:16 tells us that the angel will shout, *"Behold the bridegroom is coming go out to meet Him!"* The trumpet will sound, waking up the living as well as the dead. What a day that's going to be when the graves begin to open up, and the dead in Christ begin to get up and go up to meet the Lord in the air.

You will not be talking about I would go to the meeting but I don't have time. You will have time for Jesus on that day but for many it will be too late. You will have time that day. Your business will take a back seat that day. The banks will not close their vaults that day. Hundred-dollar bills will be floating up and down the streets that day and no one will pick up a bill. Sinner will be running but they will not find a hiding place. Mountains will move that day. The ABC liquor store with all those bars to keep folks out, will not even close the door on that day and no one will go in and get themselves a bottle. Liars will stop telling lies on that day: no one will have time to listen. Thieves will stop stealing on that day because no one will buy your stolen goods any more.

When the cry was made behold the bridegroom is coming, all the wise virgins arose and trimmed their lamps. You see in those days the groom would come to get His bride before they were married, and they would march together to the place where the wedding would take place. They didn't have automobiles and cell phones. The virgins job would be to light the pathway as they traveled to the place to be married. The wise, were ready, just waiting for the time. You know Jesus said *be* also ready for you don't know the day or the hour when the Son of Man comes back. You know you must be ready, because if you are not ready, you will not have time to get ready. Because Jesus the Savior of the world, would have gone out of the saving business, and is now sitting in the judgment seat, and all nation are now gathered before Him to be judged. You'll be like the foolish virgins who messed around, putting it off until another day, and keep on putting it off until it's a little too late.

Here comes the foolish. Give us some of your oil because our lamps are gone out. As I said before, the oil represents righteousness and you can't loan or borrow righteousness. So they were told go to them that sell and buy yourself some oil. They left in a hurry, they found some oil and came back and knocked on the door. But as fast as they could find oil and get back to the wedding was not fast enough. Why were they on the outside when they were supposed to be on the inside? They messed around, they put it off, and before they knew it, it was too late to get in. You don't want to sit around, and mess around, and put it off, like those foolish virgins and wait too late. You have these golden opportunities get yourself ready to meet the bridegroom when he comes. Because if you fool around, and put your salvation off until it's too late, you'll have to spend eternity in the wrong place. And although all your friends might be there with you, you will not want to be in that place. It is a terrible place to be in the first place, but to have to stay there forever, should remind you just how important it is to get prepared. God will give you another kind of body that will not burn up: on the contrary, it will just burn and burn and burn forever! You don't want to fool around, putting off your salvation until it's too late only to find yourself in a lake of fire, burning, and burning forever. Where every day will be a hot day. If you have a chair to sit on it will be a hot chair. If you have a bed to lay on it will be a hot bed. No one will say to you what a fine day this is. Because there will be no good days in hell.

I'm glad today to give you some good news. The good news is, that everything that needs to be done so you can enjoy eternity with God, has already been done. You just need to come give your life to the Lord. 2 Peter 3:9 tells us that God does not want us to be lost, that's why Jesus came into this world. But you need to come and give your life to Jesus. *"Come unto me,"* said Jesus, *"all that are heavy laden I will give you rest."* But you have to come. *"Behold I stand at the door and knock if any man will open up I will come in."* But you have to come to him. I'm begging you this morning come to Jesus before it's too late.

Chapter 7

BAPTISM

IN KEEPING WITH GOD'S WORD, THE BIBLE SAYS IN Ephesians. 4:4 there is one body in God plan to save man. It is a spiritual body that is the church that belongs to Jesus. Ephesians 1:22 tells us that God put all things under the feet of Christ, and gave him to be the head over all things, to the church which is His body. In this one body, which is the church, there is one Holy Spirit keeping the church alive spiritually. There is one Lord, who is the owner, He is the procurator, and He is the Savior of His body. He is Jesus the Son of God. In this one spiritual body there is one faith, Romans 10:17 tells us that this one faith comes from hearing and believing the word of God. Then there is one baptism in God's plan to save man.

This Morning We Want to Talk About Baptism

The bible teaches in Romans 15: 4 that things that were written before our time, were written for our learning. According to 1 Corinthians 10:1-2 God used baptism to sanctify His people even under the old covenant. When Paul wrote to the church in Corinth he said to them, moreover brethren I don't want you to be ignorant, you need to know that all our fathers were under the cloud and all passed through the sea, and all were baptized unto Moses in the cloud and in the sea. Baptism is a major doctrine in the bible. Those who teach a doctrine, that minimizes the important role baptism plays in our salvation, are teaching false doctrine.

Before Jesus begin His ministry and before Jesus built His church, God used baptism to get the people ready for the Church of Christ. God sent John the baptizer out to preach (Matthew 3:1). His message was repent ye for the kingdom of heaven is at hand. John preached prepare ye the way of the Lord and make His path straight. Then went out to all of Jerusalem and all Judea, and all the region round about Jordan, and were baptized by John confessing their sins. John's baptism got them ready, prepared them for Jesus. Luke said in Luke 1:17 That John went out before Jesus, to turn the hearts of the father to the children, and the disobedient to the wisdom of the just, to make ready a people prepared for the Lord. After Jesus was baptized by John, Jesus began to preach the same message that John preached. And He baptized people. Matthew. 4: 17 explains that Jesus did the preaching and His disciples did the baptizing. If you will notice in John 4:2, that John's baptism didn't put anyone in the church, and it was not for the forgiveness of sin, all John's baptism did was get them ready for the kingdom. That is why Acts 19:1-5 teaches that the people John baptized had to be *re-baptized* to get into the church.

When Jesus came to this earth, he came to give His life so that we could have everlasting life. The devil didn't know that. He's a smart fellow, but he didn't know that. He thought he knew everything but he didn't know that. The bible says in 1 Corinthians 2:7-9 the apostles wrote, "*We speak the wisdom of God in a mystery, which God ordained for our glory before the foundation of the world. Which none of the princes of this world knew: for had they known, they would not have crucified the Lord of glory.*" I know the devil was mighty happy when they put Jesus on the cross. Can't you see him jumping up and down shouting I got him now? You see the nature of the devil is to destroy: it is to tear up and hurt God's people. You know he was a happy creature when they hung Jesus up. But that was Friday and even though it did look like it was all over, it wasn't. You remember what David said sorrow may last for a night, but joy comes in the morning. Early that Sunday morning while it was still dark some angels came down and rolled the stone away, and Jesus got up, and God gave Him all power, all authority in heaven and on the earth. And He built His church.

The first thing He said when He met His disciples was, "*all power in heaven and on earth has been given to me. And now I want you to go and teach all nations. Baptizing them in the name of the father, the Son and the Holy Ghost"* (Matthew. 28:18). Mark makes it a little plainer for us, he tells us what to teach, when he said in Mark 16:15-16 go into all the world and preach the gospel to every creature, he that believe and is baptized shall be saved. You can see that one of the conditions of salvation is, you must be baptized.

One of the things we need to look at is who needs to be baptized. Let me say here little babies and infants have no need to be baptized, because the religion of Christianity is a teaching process. This means men must be taught. In John 6:45 Jesus said they shall all be taught of God, everyone who has heard and learned of the father cometh unto me. The command Jesus gave is go teach all nations and baptized them. Who are the them, those who have been taught. So until children are old enough to be taught, old enough to learn about Jesus, old enough to believe in Jesus, and come to Jesus to be baptized, they are not fit subjects for baptism. After all baptism is for the forgiveness of sin, so what willful sins have babies committed? 1 John 3:4 sin is a transgressing of God's law. It's breaking God's law and babies can't do that. In Matthew 18:3 Jesus teaches, when an old man becomes a Christian, he becomes what a little baby already is.

The bible teaches in three ways. It teaches by commands: there is a command from Jesus to be baptized. The bible teaches by examples. Let's look at how the apostles did it. Acts 2:36, when Peter was preaching, and he told them, *"You crucified the Son of God."* They didn't wait until he got through, they stopped him in the middle of his lesson. They hollered out men and brethren what shall we do. Listen to what Peter who was guided by the Holy Spirit told them to do to be saved. He said, "Repent!" Everyone who wants to go to heaven needs to repent and be baptized, by the authority of Jesus Christ and they shall receive the gift of the Holy Spirit. Those that received God's word were baptized. This is the beginning of the Lord's church. You can see the church began to grow. There were only 12 people in the church at that time. But when three thousand were baptized, there were 3,012 people that belong to God. God put them in the church that belonged to Jesus. They didn't join the church: God *added* them to His family. You have to be baptized to get in the Lord's church.

When Jesus talked about baptism, He used the flood in Noah's day to stress how important baptism is. He said in 1 Peter 3:18-21, Jesus suffered once for sin. The just for the unjust that he might bring us to God. That he was put to death in the flesh but quickens in the spirit, and that he preached to the spirits in prison, while the ark was being prepared. Where eight souls were saved by water, and the like figure where in baptism does also now save us.

You can't be saved before you are baptized, because baptism is for something, it is by something, and it's into something. We have to be baptized to be born again. Remember it's a spiritual birth into a spiritual kingdom. You can't be saved without being born again. And you can't be born again without being baptized so you must be baptized to be saved.

The story about a man named Nicodemus is found in John 3:1-7. Jesus told this man that he must be born again. The man had a hard time believing Jesus because he was an old man, and he was not thinking about a spiritual birth, but Jesus had him to understand that he was talking about a spiritual birth into a spiritual body.

I said baptism is for something. Acts 2:38 says baptism is for the forgiveness of past sins. You can't be saved in your sins, and you can't get rid of your sins without being baptized. So you must be baptized in order to be saved. I said baptism it is by something. Paul wrote in 1 Corinthians 12:12-13 *for as the body is one and have many members, and all the member being many are one body, so also is Christ, for by one spirit, are we all baptized into one body.* It is by the direction of the Holy Spirit that we are led to the water to be baptized, and it is by one spirit we are all baptized into one body.

Baptism is into something. Everyone knows that salvation is in Christ Jesus. No one believes you can be saved on the outside of Christ. So in order to be saved you must get where salvation is. 2 Timothy 2:10 tell us that salvation is in Christ. So then, what we need to know is how do I get in Christ where salvation is. Look at Galatians 3:26-27. We are all the children of God. He's talking to Christians now all Christians are children of God by faith in Christ Jesus. Now how did they get in Christ? Verse 27 for as many of you as have been baptized (INTO) Christ have put on Christ. How did they get in Christ? (THEY WERE BAPTIZED) let me say it again, no one can be saved without being baptized.

But what about the mode of baptism? What do you do when you baptize someone? Do you give them a choice as to which mode they want you to use? Usually it's a choice of three: sprinkling, pouring, or immersion. Now if they chose sprinkling, then which part of the body do you sprinkle? Since there is no example in the New Testament where any one was sprinkled, do you sprinkle the feet, the hand, or the head? Listen, the New Testament was written in Greek. The Greek word for baptism is "baptizo, which means to plunge, to dip or immerse.

Thank God, He left us an example in the book. How did the preachers and the Apostles do it in the beginning of the church? In Acts 8 Phillip, a gospel preacher, went down to the city of Samaria and preach Christ to them. What a time they were having everyone was obeying the gospel. Phillip was having great success. But God sent an angel to tell Phillip about a man, one man who needed to be baptized. You see everyone needs to be baptized. The story starts in Act 8:26. Let's look at it. The man was taught about the death and resurrection of Jesus. He was taught about baptism. He wanted to be baptized. When the preacher baptized him, they, the preacher, and the man went down into the water. The preacher didn't baptize his head or his feet, he baptized the whole body. They both went down into the water. He buried him in water like Colossians. 2:12 teaches. The preacher baptized the man not with water but in water. In Colossians 2:7 Paul told the church you've been rooted and grounded in the faith, beware, be careful that you don't be spoil through the philosophy and vain deceit of men. He told them you've been circumcised with the circumcision not made with hands. You've been buried with Christ in baptism. So you can see that people that were baptized in the New Testament were dipped, they were immersed, they were buried or covered up.

In Romans 6:17 Paul said but God be thanked that you were the servants of sin, but you have obeyed from the heart that form of doctrine, which was delivered to you. A form is a pattern that you shape things by. The form is not the real thing, but it shapes the real thing. If you want some concrete steps, you build a form, you pour the wet cement into the form, and that shapes the steps. When the steps get dry, you knock the form away. What form was delivered to them? The same form that was delivered to us. It was the gospel of Christ. What did Paul preach to them? The death burial and resurrection of Jesus. 1 Corinthians 15:1 we must obey that. Romans 6:1 teaches us how it's done.

Chapter 8

GOD'S PEOPLE DEVELOPING WATER-WALKING FAITH

(MATTHEW 14:27)

THE WORD DEVELOP MEANS TO CHANGE IN character, it means to become bigger and better, more improved and more useful. All Christians start out in an undeveloped state. But by feasting on spiritual food, as Peter said, In 1 Peter 2:2 desire the sincere milk of the word that you may grow. So you can see that by allowing God's word to guide and direct us, by feasting on God's word we develop into the kind of people that God want us to become. We develop the kind of faith that God appreciates. So we can do the kind of work that glorifies God.

And when we talk about water-walking faith. We are not talking about any one thing, but we are talking about the whole system of faith. We are talking about listening to Jesus, and believing that if Jesus said do it, no matter what it is, we can do it. It's believing that if Jesus said it will happen, we believe it as if it has already happened. Like Peter in John 21:6 when Jesus died on the cross Peter said, "I think I'll go fishing." The rest of the disciples said I'll go with you. Now they had fished all night and caught nothing. When they came in that morning, Jesus was standing on the bank. They didn't know that it was Jesus; to them it was just a man standing on the bank. Jesus asked them do you have any meat or have you caught anything? They said no. Jesus said to them cast the net on the right side of the ship. Now notice please, they didn't go into all the objections we have. Peter didn't say why the right, the left side is just as good as the right. Peter said to him we fished all night and caught nothing but at thy word we'll do it. When they obeyed the words of Jesus, they caught so many fish they couldn't pull their net in.

All children of God need water-walking faith. Because you have to take some stuff sometime that the devil's folk don't have to take. You can't take your fist and go up side a person's head like the devil's folk can, all you can do is pray for him and let God take care of him. Your burdens get heavy sometime, and you have to go through some stuff and you wonder why is it that you are trying to do the right thing. You try to live the Christians life and you still have to go through some stuff. Now you may think yourself to be a good Christian. I don't doubt that. But you are not 100 per cent until you go through some stuff and come through it better instead of being bitter. Use your faith as a stepping-stone to higher ground. You know it's like gold. It's not pure gold until it goes through the fire.

We need water-walking faith when our children will not obey the rules of our house and get all rebellious and uncontrollable. When we confront them they tell us they're going to leave. The hurting part is not that they are leaving, because there comes a time in all children's lives that they need to leave. As the song says when that old boy gets away from here we are going to make love in the kitchen. So the fact that they are leaving is not the problem. The problem is, they think that leaving will hurt us, they just want to hurt us, and they are unaware of the fact that they are hurting themselves.

We need water-walking faith when someone tells one of those hurting lies on you and everyone including your own wife believes it to be true. Yet, you know that you've done no wrong.

We need water-walking faith when it seem like the devil's folk are having such a good time doing what they do. They try to tempt us to join them. They say, don't knock it until you try it; because when you try it you'll like it. So don't try it. All sin is enjoyable for a season until it's time to pay the piper; till it's time to suffer the consequences of your actions. It's like borrowing money; it's easy to get but hard to pay back. Permit me to talk to the young people for a little while. The worst reason to do anything is because someone else is doing it. Don't start sucking on beer bottles just because others are doing it. And it seem to us that we are having such a hard time, even after all our praying, and praising God, and trying to live a righteous life. I tell you that we do need water-walking faith.

By Way of Introduction

When we look at the story of Peter walking on the water, Jesus had just fed 5,000 men with two fish and five loaves of bread. And according to John 6:15 when the people saw this, they wanted to take Jesus by force, and make him their king. Jesus knew what they were planning to do, so Matthew 14:22 says that Jesus commanded them (the disciples) or constrained them to get into the ship and go to the other side of the lake. And then he sent the people away. And he himself went up into a mountain to pray. Mark said, in Mark 6:47 when the evening was come, the ship was in the middle of the sea. And Jesus saw them toiling, underscore the words Jesus saw them. He was not with them in the boat, but rather he saw them. They were having a hard time. But he was watching them. No one had high-powered motors on their boats at that time. They were rowing with their hands against the wind. It was a stormy night and the sea was raging, the wind was blowing hard against them. But they didn't turn back.

Remember now, it was a good day when they left headed to the other side. But somewhere between where they left from, and where they were trying to get they ran into a storm. And I can tell you that somewhere between where you are now and where you are trying to get you will run into a storm. But listen to this, because Jesus told them to go to the other side, they didn't think about turning back. Were they struggling? Yes. Were they afraid? Yes. Were they making no progress? No. But they were not about to turn around. Whatever you do when the contrary winds of life begin to blow against you don't turn around. Hang in there. Put your anchors down and just stay there. Don't ever doubt God. And don't forget that sometimes the Lord will let you struggle, and agonize for a while before he will come and rescue you. He was watching over them all the time like a mother watches over her child. So when you are being tried by the devil, just remember that Jesus is watching. As David said in the long ago, sorrow may last for a night, but joy cometh in the morning. There is a need for us to learn how to hold on until the morning. The bible says it was in the fourth watch of the night. about three o clock in the morning. They looked up and in the midst of those waves they saw the appearance of a man walking on the water. They had never seen or heard about anyone walking on water. They thought it must be a ghost. Notice please that Jesus came walking on the very thing that was giving them a problem. Problems mean nothing to Jesus. He creates problems, and he solves problems, sometimes He has to give us a problem so that He can get our attention. Do you ever, when things are going bad for you, take a retrospect look back in your life, and say maybe it's my fault all this stuff is happening to me? Maybe God is trying to get my attention so I need to do better. Sometimes the Lord has to close some windows so He can open some doors for us. We need to remember that Jesus is Lord over nature. That He treads upon the sea, and rides upon the wind. And nothing is impossible for Him. Remember it was dark. And they couldn't see who it was. They were shaking in their boots like Jell-O, when you drop it on the floor. Jesus had to hurry and speak don't be afraid it's me. Peter said to Him, *"Lord, if it is you."* Peter still had some doubts in his mind. If it is you, let me come to you on the water. As I told you before, when Jesus tells you to do something you can do it. Because he'll help you do it.

Can't you see Peter in your mind? Slowly climbing over the side of the boat. Holding on making sure he didn't fall. After a while his feet touched the water, and he noticed he didn't sink. The same power that made iron swim for the prophet, the same power that cause the Red Sea to divide for Moses, the same power that made the Jordan river to dry up for Joshua, the same power that allowed a dead man do get up out of his tomb, enabled Peter to walk on the water.

Here he goes, doing the impossible, walking on the water going to meet Jesus. But remember as I told you that it was a stormy night and the sea was raging. The waves were jumping high. And Peter was doing all right until he began to worry about the stormy sea he was in. When he took his eyes off Jesus and his thoughts turned to the waves he began to sink.

Whenever you find yourself in the middle of a storm. Keep your eyes on Jesus. And you know that sometimes storms rise up in the church. That's why you need water-walking faith, so you will not get blown away. It's no time to run, but it is time to anchor down in prayer, and renew your faith in Christ. When your faith gets weak, your prayers should get strong. And don't forget that the sinking of our spirits is caused by the weakness of our faith.

So I say to you this morning as you try to make your journey from earth to heaven, keep your eyes on Jesus. All things are possible if you only believe. Storms will come up in every one's life every now and then, but keep your eyes on Jesus. And don't ever forget that if they lied on Jesus they surely will lie on you. You need water-walking faith when your neighbor is unfriendly, hard to get along with and mean. You need water-walking faith, when the people who used to love you so much, allow that love to turn to hate. You need to develop water-walking faith, so when the doctors begin to tell you everything but what you want to hear, you can keep your eyes on Jesus. You need water-walking faith so when you have to take your loved one to the cemetery and leave them there, you can keep your eyes on Jesus. You need water-walking faith so if your wife or husband just will not do right, you can keep your eyes on Jesus. You need to have water-walking faith when your children do everything but what you want them to do.

If you keep your eyes on Jesus, you'll have no problem setting your affection on the things above and not on the things of this earth. And holding on to God's unchanging hands. As the old folks use to say let's walk together children and don't get weary, there's a great camp meeting at the end of the day. You will be going to a place where the winds don't blow and the thunders don't roar. God will give you a new body that will not grow old and will never wear out. We are going to a family reunion that will last and last and last. We are going to a place where the glory of God will light up the place. We'll sing a new song as we gather around the throne of God. No wonder John wrote blessed are the dead that die in the Lord, the spirit said we'll rest from our labors. Do yourself a favor this morning and come to Jesus and let Him get you ready for that great day and do your best to develop water-walking faith.

Chapter 9

PATIENCE

"IT'S SUCH A BLESSING, PLUS AN HONOR FOR ME TO be at Beach Island today. God is so good, and so full of grace and mercy until He granted me this opportunity for us to worship together today. I need to say a great big thank you to your fine minister, Moses Johnson, for inviting me to come."

"Your minister, Moses Johnson, reminds me of Jonah, who tried to go everywhere but where God wanted Him to go. You know the story of Jonah how God prepared a great fish, and had the fish to swallow Jonah. God knew where he needed to be. And when Jonah got out of that fish belly it didn't take him long to get where God wanted him to be. Moses tried his best not to become the minister of this church, but God knew that's where he needed to be. The church is being blessed, and God wants the church to bless brother Moses, work with him, treat him with respect, and God will do the rest."

Far too many times in our lifetime we are made to feel sad, and we have unhappy days and sleepless nights, all because of what someone said, or tried to do to us. We've been lied on and mistreated many times in our lives, and most time we acted or reacted in the wrong way. The aim of our lesson today is to show by the scriptures, that there is power and a blessing in the ability to be patient, and to suffer without complaining, while being mistreated, if we can maintain the right spirit.

The way God wants us to live seems hard to us, only because we haven't made up our minds to suffer for the cause for which Christ died. Jesus suffered a whole lot of mistreatment because of us, and we should be willing to suffer for His cause.

There is a blessing that the God of heaven will give to all who maintain the right attitude and the right spirit toward their fellow Christians, and to God, even while they are being persecuted. It's unreal anyway for us to believe that we can live in this world and never be lied on, never be talked about in an evil way, and never be mistreated. And there is something wrong with us if, every time someone say something evil about us, we go all to pieces. If you are a Christian, you expect that. All of that comes with the territory. It's like being a football player. When you get the ball, you expect to be knocked down. It's just wishful thinking for a football player to think he can play football without being knocked down. And it makes no sense for a Christian to believe that he or she can live in the kind of world we live in and never be mistreated. Paul said in 2 Timothy 3:12 all who live Godly in Christ Jesus shall suffer persecution. You will be persecuted. (SHALL) is used in the place of will, its future tense meaning it will happen. Some of us don't do things we know we should do all because we don't want to be talked about.

But Jesus pronounced a blessing upon all His people when they can maintain the right spirit, and the right attitude, while being persecuted. Listen to Jesus as he talks to His disciples in Matthew 5:11-12. *"Blessed are you,"* He said, *"when men shall revile you, say bad things about you, tell lies on you to make others dislike you, and persecute you, going all out of their way to do you wrong. And say all kinds of evil things about you."* Jesus said, instead of feeling bad about it, instead of feeling sad about it, instead of wanting to cuss him out, instead of wanting to knock them out, instead of planning to even up the score, Jesus said, "Rejoice!" Be happy about it.

It's shouting time when we have the opportunity to suffer like Jesus had to suffer for us. It's shouting time when we are called upon to go the extra mile for Jesus, because this will give us a greater reward in heaven. That is, if you can suffer without complaining, and if you can maintain the right spirit while you suffer. The enemy can't understand why you don't get upset and act all unchristian like when they do and say things designed to mess up your spirit. It's like graduating from high school. All will graduate, but a few will graduate with honors.

My subject this morning is Patience. The idea for this lesson comes from Romans 5:1-5. Patience has always played a great role in God's plan to save man. God had tolerance and patience with the children of Israel when they wouldn't obey Him. On one occasion he allowed His people, the children of Israel, to be in slavery and they had to serve another nation for over 400 years. And after they crossed the sea, they wouldn't obey God, and they had to march around in the wilderness for another 40 years. In like manner, God has patience with us. He tolerates all our sinful doing, and still wakes us up on time every morning. That is, until Sunday morning. He must be a little slow on Sunday morning, because some of us just can't get here on time.

We know how many times in our lifetime we sinned against God. Yes, we know how much wrong we've done over our lifetime. And we know that the only reason we are blessed to be in Christ today, is because of God's patience with us. God tolerated and put up with all our wrongdoing for such a long time because He knew what we would become. I understand better now what David meant when he said, in Psalms 73:2 my feet were almost gone. Some of us can testify to the fact that God got a hold on us just in the nick of time. What are you saying preacher? I'm trying to show you, how God put up with all our wrongdoing, for such a long time because He loves us, and because He knows what we will become. We have to tolerate each other's mistakes and try to help each other overcome our mistakes. That's what Jesus meant when He said love one another as I have loved you, and by this men will know that you belong to me. That is what Paul meant when he said in Philippians 2:3-4, let nothing be done through strife, or vainglory. But in lowliness of mind, let each of you esteem others better than yourself. He said, look not every man on the things of his own, but look after the things of others. And you know that if you are looking out for me, and I'm looking out for you, she's looking out for him, he's looking out for her, everybody is looking out for everybody, no one will go lacking. But we are talking about patience.

We live in a busy hurried world, a world where we constantly come in contact with people. Each one has his or her own unique appearance, personality, and their own way of doing things. Because of the quick pace of our lives, and the difference in human nature, which we daily encounter, we often find our tempers rising, our blood boiling, and our irritation showing all because things don't happen like we think they should. What we need more than anything else is a double portion of the old-fashioned virtue call patience. Now this is especially true for Christians, who must let their light shine at all time. The light of an angry, impatient, Christian does not glow.

When we talk about patience, we are talking about being able to bear or endure pain, stand up under trails and criticism, without complaining. It means suffering a long time under provocation, being undisturbed by obstacles that are put in our way by others. It means being calm in the face of all provocation. In Ephesians 4:1-2 Paul said I beg you that you walk worthy of the vocation where in you are called. With all lowness, and meekness, with longsuffering. William Barclay, theologian and Professor of Divinity and Biblical Criticism at the University of Glasgow commented on the word longsuffering said, it's the spirit that bears the sheer foolishness of men, without irritation. It's the spirit that can suffer unpleasant people with graciousness and fools without complaints.

Patience is one of the things that become sound doctrine. All Christians need patient. And every one needs to be a Christian. Now you don't have to beg God to save you, God want you saved. God keeps all His promises. That's why Jesus died on a cross so you can be saved. Peter said in 2 Peter 3:9 God is not willing that any should perish, but that all should come to repentance. Titus 2: 1-2 Paul told the young preacher to speak the things that become sound doctrine. And this is what he told him to teach. Tell the aged men to be sober, grave, and temperate, be sound in faith, in love and patient. It is one of the virtues that the preacher is commanded to have (1 Timothy 6:11). The preacher was told to flee worldly things, and follow after righteousness, meekness, faith and patience. It is a virtue that must be practiced without respect of person. We must be patience toward all men. Many of the Old Testament men were known for their patience. Remember the patience of Job has become a proverb among bible believing people.

Let us listen to a man who experienced much suffering in his life-time. The apostle Paul, he was hated by his former friends when he became a Christian. He was beaten and put in jail, and finally killed. Paul was not the only one who tried to convince us to believe that whatever happened to us bad, is nothing but a stepping stone to a blessing from God if we learn how to suffer without complaining, while maintaining the right attitude and keeping the right spirit. Listen to James the brother of Jesus. James 1:2 He said my brethren count it all joy when you fall into many temptations, know this, that the trying of your faith works patience.

Paul said in Romans 5:3 but we rejoice in tribulations also. We rejoice in the Lord, we should rejoice when all is well, and rejoice when all is not well. We are not only happy we are in fellowship with God, and have communion with Him daily, but we rejoice in tribulations also. If we could get it through our head, that all the suffering we endure because we are children of God, are sanctified by the grace of God, and has the power to increase our blessing from God. Jesus said in Luke 21:19 in your patience you possess your soul. You preserve your soul. You bless your soul, and cause it to prosper when you have patience.

If you could just learn how to keep a calm temper when you hear what they say about you. And what you know they tried to do to you. If we will be willing to suffer without complaining or being discontented while maintaining the right spirit, we will indeed be blessed. We need to be able to say I'll put it in God's hand, and I'll let God handle it. And when you put it in God's hands let it stay there. I'll put my trust in the fact that God is able to take care of me and keep on marching up the king's highway. Whatever others say about us, whatever others try to do to us, is just more stars in our crown. This kind of attitude will get us to God's house in style. I'm reminded of the crying prophet, found in Jeremiah 18:1 God told him go down to the potter's house. He needed to stop all that crying, go down to the potter's house, and watch him work. God wanted him to learn a lesson from the potter. God told him, Watch the potter as he puts wet clay on the wheel to make a vessel to please him. Pay attention to the fact that the clay has no mind of its own; the clay does not move until the potter moves it. Whatever the potter decided to make out of the clay, is all right with the clay. And sometimes the potter will make a vessel that doesn't turn out just right, he doesn't throw it away, he just smashes it down, and starts all over, working with it until he gets it right. He'll start all over shaping it until he gets it right.

And God told Jeremiah, My people are just like clay in the potter's hand. God is the potter you know. God has the power to make us what he wants us to be, if we would be like clay in His hands. We may not turn out right the first time, but if we let Him, He'll keep on working with us until He get us right. And I'm so glad that God is not through with us yet. He's still working with us. We may not be all that God wants us to be right now, but we can thank God we are not what we use to be. Be sure you move by God's orders. God is not through with us yet. He is still working with us, He

Patience

want us to become what He wants us to be. So He gives us the power to become. There is a story I love to tell about Peter. When they arrested Jesus, Peter followed a long ways off. He stayed out of sight. When he got to the place where they were trying Jesus, they had shut the door. John had the doorkeeper to open the door and let Peter in. A little girl asked him are you one of His disciples? He said no. He lied. The man, to whom Jesus promised to give the keys of the kingdom, lied. But Jesus knew before He promised to give Peter the keys that Peter would become a liar. His grace and His mercy allowed Him to put up with Peter's lying, because He knew what Peter would become. The only reason God puts up with our foolishness, and tolerates all our wrong-doing, is because He knows what we will become for Him. It was cold that night. And the enemy had made a fire and Peter was warming himself by their fire. After a while another man saw him and asked are you one of them? Peter said I don't know the man. But after a while, someone said to him you are one of them, your speech betrays you. (In other words, you sound just like one of those old Church of Christ folk. And he begins to lie and cuss. Jesus just looks at him and he went to crying. He repented. But Peter thought that because of what he'd done, Jesus couldn't use him anymore. So he said I think I'll go fishing. And the other disciples said we'll go with you. You know the story; they fished all night and caught nothing. When they got back to the bank Jesus was standing on the bank. But they didn't know that it was Jesus. He asked them, have you caught anything? They said no. Jesus said cast your net on the right side of the boat. When they did what Jesus told them to do, they caught more fish than they'd ever caught in their fishing career. The net was not designed to hold that many fish. So John hollered out, it's the Lord!

Jesus asked Peter, Peter do you love me. Peter said yes Lord. Jesus said I need you to feed my sheep. Don't worry about the fact that you've been cussing and lying. I forgave you of that when you repented. All I want you to do now is feed my sheep. My grace and my mercy will take you the rest of the way. Let me say it one more time if you will. I'm so glad that God is not through with us yet. He still needs us to feed His sheep. His grace and His mercy have made us free. We are like mountain climbers for the Lord. And you know how mountain climbers always put the man with the most experience in front. And they tie themselves together with the same rope. And they have to look out for each other, because if one falls they all fall because they are tied together. And on this spiritual journey, we are all tied together with a spiritual rope. And we must look out for each other because if we are not careful and fail to stand together we will all go down together. As Paul said long ago, in Philippians 3:13 brethren I count not myself to have appended. He saying there are some things I don't understand yet. But there's one thing I've learn to do. I'm forgetting those things that are behind, and I press on toward the mark of God in Christ Jesus. That's good advice for all of us. Because we need to let the past stay where it need to stay, and that's in the past.

Chapter 10

RIGHTLY DIVIDING

THE IDEA FOR THIS LESSON COMES FROM 2 Timothy 2:14-15 rightly dividing the word of God. There are at least four different reasons why people come to worship service. Some want to be able to say I went to worship service today. They don't get involved in nothing. They are the don't bother me Christians, I gave my 15 cent and I'll see you next Sunday. Some come expecting an emotional high. They want to be made to cry, and that makes them feel like the Lord worked with them in a special way. Some come and they listen real well. But they are not listening to learn how to improve their spiritual life, they are picky Christians, they pick out everything that might be used against someone else. But thank God, some come to learn. They come hungering and thirsting after righteousness, they just want to know what right is, and they intend to do it.

Rightly Dividing the Word of God

The apostle Paul is writing a letter to the young preacher Timothy. Telling him to do your best to present yourself to God, as one approved, being a workman who does not need to be ashamed, And one who correctly handles the word of truth. When we talk about truth, we are talking about being in accord with what is, what was, and what must be. The truth means telling it like it is without adding anything to it or taking anything from it. The truth is important in every realm of life, but it is especially important in religion. And how we worship God. Because if we fail to practice religion according to the truth of God's word, then we are practicing religion in vain. Now the aim of this lesson is to show by the scriptures that, if we fail to study and understand the scriptures correctly, we will get involved in a misunderstanding of the scriptures. And we will not know what to do to be saved, and how to do what God told us to do. I think I need to tell you that you can do what God told you to do, and fail to do it like God told you to do it, and God will not accept it.

In the beginning of the bible, God warns us, Deuteronomy 4:2 God told Moses to tell the children of Israel you shall not add unto the word which I command you, neither shall ye diminish aught from it, that you may keep the commandments of the Lord your God. You can't keep the commandments of God, adding to or taking from God's word. In the middle of the bible, Proverbs 30:6, God tells us to add thou not unto God's words lest he reprove thee and thou be found to be a lie. In the end of the bible, the last chapter of the bible and the last verse of the bible before the benediction, He warns not to add. Listen to this. Revelations 22:18 *for I testify unto every man that hear the words of the prophecy of this book If any man add unto these things, God shall add unto him the plagues that are written in this book. And if any man shall take away from the words of the book of this prophecy, God shall take away His part out of the book of life, and out of the holy city, and from the things that are written in this book.* It's mighty important that we follow instructions from God on how to be saved, and what to do to be saved.

The aim of this lesson today is to show by the scriptures that God didn't leave us on our own to try to figure out how to get to heaven. God didn't command the preachers to figure out how to get to heaven. All He told the preacher to do is go into all the world and preach my word, the gospel, to every creature. Preachers have no business preaching stuff that God didn't say. God left us direct commands. And good instructions and all the information we need, that tells us what to do to get to heaven. And He even left us instructions on how to do what He told us to do. Because you can do what God told you to do, and do it the wrong way and He will not accept it.

The aim of this lesson is to show you that if you fail to rightly divide God's word, you'll wind up with a big misunderstanding of what God wants you to do. We want to show you that there is a standard of authority set forth by God, to help us rightly divide His word. Peter wrote a letter to the church. In 1 Peter 1:20 he said, in order to rightly divide God's word you need to know this first. He said no scripture is of any private interpretation. Every one needs to know that scriptures interpret scriptures, and that there's no such thing taught in the bible as you have your understanding of it, and I have another understanding of the same thing. Because all of us know that there is but one right way to understand a thing, and all who understand it will understand it the same way.

Two plus two equals 4. Is there another way to understand that? No a thousand times no. If you come up with any number other than four you don't have another understanding of it, you have a misunderstanding of it. Anytime you have one scripture contradicting another scripture your understanding of it is wrong. Let us look at a verse in the bible that's misquoted, misunderstood and wrongly applied by most people. We have far too many people talking about I got saved way back when. Read Mark 16:15-16. It says, " he that believe." That's no 1. And is baptized, shall be saved. Shall be is future tense. You are not saved now; the only thing you are saved from now is past sins. But you will be saved. No one who is alive today is already saved. Past tense. So when you believe and are baptized, you are in a safe state. And if you die in that state you shall be saved, Future tense.

Now let's look at something else about this verse. Read it once more. Did that say anything about praying and getting a religion? Did that say anything about joining the church of your choice? The instructions here are plain. You need to follow God's instructions. There are some things that you have to follow instruction or it will not work. All of us drive a car. You know what the instructions are, put water in the radiator, oil in the crank case and gas in the gas tank. Now you can do it another way but your car will not run.

Rightly Dividing the Word of God

Now let's talk about the bible for a moment. Because you have to have confidence in the bible as God's word. That is, if you intend to spend eternity with God you must believe that this book contains the words of God. It's the mind of God reveal to man. Everything God intended for us to believe, obey, and practice in religion is found in this book. You can't afford to be talking about Paul wrote this and this is just Paul talking. You got to believe that it's God talking. Because all of the bible came directly from heaven. We must teach the bible, not our opium. We must believe the bible. It not what we think, it's not our opinion, and it's certainly not our philosophy, that's going to get us into heaven, it's what the bible teach that will get us into heaven. The bible is the mind of God reveal to man. It tells us how God thinks and was design to change our thinking and cause us to think like God. Everything God want us to know about Him, everything God want us to believe about Him. Everything God want us to do, and the way he want us to do it, is found in the bible. The bible contains the mind of God, the state of man, the way of salvation, the doom of sinners and the happiness of the believers. The bible. Its doctrines are holy, its histories are true. You need to read it to be wise, how many of you open your bibles since last Sunday? You need to believe it to be safe, and practice it to be holy. It contains light to direct you, spiritual food to support you, and comfort to cheer you up. The bible. It is the traveler's map, the pilgrim's staff, the pilot's compass, the soldier's sword, and the Christian's charter. The bible should fill our memory, it should rule our hearts and guide our feet. But if you fail to rightly divide it, you will not understand how to play your part in your salvation. The bible is divided up into two dispensations; call the Old Testament and the New Testament. And I believe that the only reason why so many earnest people who really want to be saved, are still walking in darkness, is because they don't understand the difference between the Old and New Testament. They don't know that salvation for us, you and I, can't be found in the Old Testament. The Old Testament tells us what God told them to do, it tells us how God dealt with them. But what God told Moses to tell the children of Israel to do, is not what Jesus told you and I to do to be saved today. The way David worshipped God is not the way Jesus wants us to worship Him today.

To rightly divide the word of God, we must recognize that some of the bible is history. The Old Testament is a history book for us. It's a true record of how God dealt with His people a long time ago. And what is said in these records were for them and not for us. The laws of the Old Testament are inadequate to govern God's people today. There never was a law needed to govern something that does not exist. And the Church of Christ did not exist in Old Testament days. So there are no laws in the Old Testament to govern the Church of Christ. How to become a Christian is not found in the Old Testament, because there were no Christians in the Old Testament dispensation. Let me show you something. Not too long ago about 100 years ago. we lived in the horse and buggy days. The laws that were in effect then would certainly not be adequate to govern us today. There were no pave roads, no speed limit signs limiting the speed to 55 miles per hour. There was nothing at that time that could run 55 miles per hour. The bible talks about the fact that the law of the Old Testament is not for the Christian. Listen, turn your bibles to Galatians 3:21 but under the Law of Moses, Jesus was not the Savior of the world. Jesus was a silent partner with God in the Old Testament, but God the Father was doing all the talking and giving all the commands. Jesus never said a word in the Old Testament. But today God is a silent partner with Jesus, and Jesus is giving all the commands. Jesus is now the Savior of the world. He left heaven to come down here to seek and save the lost. But he plans to save the lost in His church. Jesus didn't have a church in the Old Testament. And since this is true, there are no laws governing the church found in the Old Testament. Jesus had to build himself a church to save us in.

Listen to Him as He gets ready to build Himself a church. Matthew 16:13-18 He asked His disciples, "Who do men say I am?" And they begin to tell Him what men said about Him. They said to Him, "Some say that you are John the Baptist. Others say that you are Elias. Some say that you are Jeremiah. Others just say that you are one of the Prophets." Didn't a single one of them know what they were talking about they were all wrong. Reminds me of people today. You tell them that Jesus has a church, and you will hear them say, child it makes no difference what church you are a member of, all churches belong to God. You don't even have to be a member of a church to be saved, others will say, (the church is in your heart) others will asked, "What about the thief on the cross?" Now here's where rightly dividing God's word is important. (1) The word of God teaches only one church, (2) the thief died before the church that belongs to Jesus was established. The thief was saved under the Law of Moses. He never was a member of a church. (3) If the church was in your heart every man and woman would have their own church. But let's go further. Listen to what Jesus says. "Who do you say that I am?" Peter spoke up; you are the Christ the Son of the living God. Jesus reminded Peter that it was God that revealed this knowledge to you. And he said upon this truth I will build my church.(I will build) does all the churches you know about belong to Jesus? Let's see if we can find out how many did Jesus build. Remember now that Jesus is the builder, the owner, the proctor and the Savior of His church. How many did He build? Verse 18 upon this rock I will build my church. Whose church is He going to build? My church. And the gates of hell shall not prevail against it. In Ephesians. 4:4 Paul put it in cement when he said there is one body. In 1 Corinthians12:12-13, 1Corithians 12:20, and Ephesians. 3:3 what is the body? Ephesians 1:22 Colossians 1:18.

Turn your bibles to Hebrews 9:15 as I close. Jesus had to die to bring the New Testament into effect. And for this cause, Jesus is the mediator of the New Testament. He had to die to bring these blessing we enjoy into being. He died not only for you and me, but He died for the redemption of the sinners that were under the first testament. The bible says that where a testament is, there must also of necessity be the death of the testator. For a testament is enforced only after men are dead.

It's like you making a will, and put all your children in your will. They can't get a thing until you die. And when you die I won't get a thing because I'm not in your family. But I came to tell you today that God has a will. And all His children are in His will. The only difference is God is not going to die, but when you die, if you are one of His children. You need to be one of His children. Because all His children will inherit eternal life. Think about it. When you die God has a blessing just waiting for you, and you need to do everything He told you to do. I want to encourage you today start today. Get in His family today.

About the Author

I.V. WHITE

I.V. WHITE IS A PREACHER. HE IS A PREACHER'S preacher. A motivator of God's people on earth. He has preached from Los Angeles, California to Miami, Floridia.

He preaches for the Haigler Street Church of Christ in Abbeville, South Carolina and is now in his fifty second year of service to the church. He has trained and sent out nine gospel preachers who is now serving different congregations.

www.ingramcontent.com/pod-product-compliance
Lightning Source LLC
Chambersburg PA
CBHW031256290426
44109CB00012B/605